M000223961

Japanese Eyes

Learning to Live in Hawai'i

American Heart

Volume III

Tendai Educational Foundation

2013

Distributed by University of Hawai'i Press

Dedicated to . . .

All who helped to shape our lives by showing us the way: mothers and fathers, grandparents, sisters and brothers, husbands and wives, daughters and sons, aunties and uncles, teachers and mentors, friends, pets…and our home, Hawai'i. To you all, a heartfelt *mahalo nui loa.*

In fond remembrance of . . .

The late U.S. Senator Daniel K. Inouye and the late Dr. George Suzuki, who began this journey with us and whose life work and spirit continued to inspire us all along the way.

Tendai Educational Foundation
Bishop Ryokan Ara, President

Publication Committee
Yoshiaki Fujitani
Fujio Matsuda
Drusilla Tanaka
Karleen Chinen, Editor

ISBN 9-780615-73366-1

This book is printed on acid-free paper and meets the guidelines for permanence and durability of the Council on Library Resources

Book design by Susan Yamamoto

MAHALO NUI LOA TO OUR SUPPORTERS

442nd Regimental Combat Team Foundation

Dr. Mary Bitterman

Gary Furugen

Honpa Hongwanji Mission of Hawaii, Social Concerns Committee

Island Insurance Foundation

Matson

Dr. George Suzuki

In Memory of Koichi and Taniyo Taniguchi,
Founders of KTA Super Stores and K. Taniguchi, Ltd.

Tendai Educational Foundation

Dr. Hideto Tomabechi

ACKNOWLEDGMENTS

Daniel Arashiro

Center for Oral History, University of Hawai'i at Mānoa

Jean Coffman

Consulate General of Japan
Yoshihiko Kamo
Toyoei Shigeeda

Hawaii's Plantation Village

Jan Mills, Hagadone Printing Company

Esther T. Mo'okini

Pacific Buddhist Academy
Pieper Toyama, Joshua Hernandez-Morse and Students

Ann Matsuda Sueoka

Japanese Eyes, American Heart

Learning to Live in Hawai'i

Volume III

TABLE OF CONTENTS

PREFACE: THE LEGACY OF THE NISEI

Bishop Ryokan Ara

President, Tendai Educational Foundation

America is a nation of immigrants. With the exception of Native Americans, who were the first to inhabit America, people from all over the world have arrived on the shores of this great nation with dreams of making it their home.

Immigrants from the European continent were the first to arrive. They worked hard and overcame many adversities, including discrimination, to build a new life in America. In time, they adapted to this new country, became citizens and began writing their history in America.

Later came immigrants from Asia, who suffered a great deal of discrimination, especially the Japanese, in their effort to become Americans. Like the Europeans before them, they sacrificed, overcame hardships and claimed America as their country.

But the history of the Japanese community is unique, for never before in America's history was one group of Americans stripped of their constitutional rights, imprisoned in camps and forced to sacrifice their young men in war to prove their loyalty to America.

This book highlights the *Nisei* generation, the American-born children of the Japanese immigrants. In fighting for the country of their birth, they fought also for the honor of their parents and to lay the foundation for a more just society for future generations.

Because of their courage and sacrifice, the future of the *Nisei* returning from the war changed dramatically, especially in Hawai'i. They and those who had remained on the home front involved themselves in education, government and

1

politics and changed the social and political landscape of Hawai'i. They assumed leadership positions in government, business and other sectors that had been closed to Americans of Japanese ancestry prior to World War II. Their success would change the face of not only Hawai'i, but America, as well.

When I think of the strength and spirit of the *Nisei*'s soul, I am reminded of a *katana*, a Japanese sword.

The Japanese sword is made through a special process of fusing metals. The center of the blade is made of malleable metal while the outer blade is made of steel. The two metals are pounded hundreds of times and fired thousands of times to create an extraordinarily strong blade.

The cross-section of the Japanese sword revealing the fusion of the two metals — one hard and strong and the other malleable and resilient — is like the strength and spirit of the *Nisei*. The character values that the *Nisei* learned from their parents, teachers, in Sunday schools and even in Japanese language schools are the malleable part of the sword. Values such as *gambari*, to persevere against all odds; *on*, a debt of gratitude in the deepest sense; *okagesama de*, acknowledgment and gratitude for the good that one has benefited from as a result of others, were lessons that Japanese immigrant parents consciously instilled in their American-born children. These values sustained the *Nisei* who went to war and gave them the courage to fight on against all odds; in every day life, it helped them to persevere in the face of adversity. These values became the heart and soul of the *Nisei* and helped them become contributing members of a global community.

The part of the sword that is hard as steel are the lessons the *Nisei* learned in their American schools — democracy, freedom, equality and, in Hawai'i, the spirit of *aloha* and love for their native home.

Today's Japanese American community is comprised of the last of the *Nisei* generation; their *Sansei*, or third-generation children; the *Yonsei* (fourth-generation Japanese American) and *Gosei* (fifth-generation Japanese American), many of whom are of mixed race. Among the younger generation, these precious values are slipping away. I believe it is important that younger generations of Japanese Americans and all young people have the opportunity to learn about the character values through the stories contained in this volume.

Toward that end, I contacted a number of *Nisei* in Hawai'i and asked them to share their experiences as they pertain to these cultural values. The first two *Nisei* I contacted were the Reverend Yoshiaki Fujitani and Dr. Fujio Matsuda, for whom I have the utmost respect.

2

I would especially like to thank them for their contributions to this publication. Both are accomplished *Nisei* who served their country in World War II and then came home to Hawai'i and served their community, remembering always the values they learned as children and applying them in their professional lives.

They did not hesitate to join me in the effort to publish this book, "Japanese Eyes, American Heart (Volume Three): Learning to Live in Hawai'i." "*Kodomo no tame ni* . . . for the sake of our children," they said. I extend my heartfelt gratitude to them.

Finally, I pray that the legacy of the *Nisei* will find its way into the heart, spirit and soul of the generations to come.

"YOU ARE ALL THE FUTURE OF HAWAI'I..."

Wallace S. Fujiyama

"Young people today are not buying what their parents and generations before them have been selling in terms of traditions and customs that are centuries-old.

"Young people of today are the first to have grown up in the affluence generated by the economic miracle of the past two decades. You know little about either the poverty of the prewar years or the suffering of the early 1900s. Moreover, you are not interested in the major traumas that your parents have gone through.

"You all have an entirely different value system from that of your parents. Your fundamental attitudes toward life are so alien to those of the older local people that we can honestly refer to you as someone from outer space.

"Having been brought up in comfort, you believe that life is basically to be enjoyed. You are not impressed by the social norms and customs of Hawai'i. You feel free to live life the way you wish, and this kind of thinking will have grave effects on every aspect of local life and the work ethic...

"You are all the future of Hawai'i. Where will your children be when they grow up? Where will you be when you get to be my age? All maids and bellhops?

"Maybe I am a voice in the dark. Hopefully, higher education is not developing a group of sheep or monkeys with all the bad Western habits.

"Hopefully, what I feel today turns out to be wrong. We need to straighten out our values or surely we will return to where we came from."

— *Source: Notes by Wallace S. "Wally" Fujiyama for a lecture to Dr. Franklin Odo's University of Hawai'i at Mānoa Ethnic Studies Class in the 1980s and 1990s.*

OKAGESAMA DE, HAWAI'I

Y. David Iha

While attending a conference in Honolulu in 1961, Dr. V. Raymond Edman, President of Wheaton College, a Christian liberal arts college in Illinois, made time in his schedule to fly to Kaua'i to meet my parents, Shigekichi and Kamato Yuki Iha. The pastor of Koloa Missionary Church drove President Edman to our old plantation home in Kōloa.

My parents, immigrants from Okinawa, Japan, were both excited and humbled that President Edman would visit with them at the home they rented from the plantation. President Edman's observation of his visit was included in his 1972 biography, "V. Raymond Edman: In the Presence of the King," by Earle E. Cairns, Professor Emeritus of Wheaton College: "A visit with the parents of David Iha, who had been the co-captain of the football team in 1960–61 was an added pleasure. This family with great effort, though of moderate income, had sent their children to college."

In truth, my family's income was hardly "moderate" — we were poor. But my parents, who spoke very little English, were steadfastly committed to giving their children a good education and worked tirelessly toward that end.

Our corrugated tin-roof plantation home in Portuguese Camp was indeed a humble one: We had neither hot, running water nor an indoor toilet. There were several "camps," or neighborhoods, like ours in Kōloa, including Spanish Camp, Japanese Camp, Filipino Camp and Banana Camp.

My *otoosan* (father), Shigekichi Iha, immigrated to Hawai'i in 1907 at age eighteen to avoid being conscripted into the Japanese army. After spending some time on O'ahu and then Maui, he made Kaua'i his home and worked as a laborer until retiring from Grove Farm Company in 1953. I'm not sure how much formal education Otoosan received in Okinawa, but I recall his friends asking him to write letters in Japanese to their families in Okinawa. Otoosan devoted his retirement years to his yard and garden. He was ninety-three years old when he died.

Okaasan — my mother, Kamato Yuki Iha — came to Kauaʻi in 1919 at the age of sixteen to help her sister, Mrs. Kama Kaneshiro, who was already living in Kōloa, care for her eleven children. Okaasan lived with the Kaneshiro family in Banana Camp, helping to clean the house, doing the laundry by hand, and taking care of her nieces and nephews.

To earn some money, Okaasan did the laundry for some of the camp bachelors, including Otoosan's. With the intervention of a few "go-betweens," they were married in 1921. Nine children followed — I was the youngest.

My parents didn't speak much English, while we children spoke mainly English and only a little Japanese or Okinawan language. Whenever they didn't want to share their conversation with us, they spoke in Okinawan. Despite our language differences, they made it clear to us through their actions that hard work and determination were worthwhile values. They said an education was critical to getting ahead and something that could never be taken away from us. Even with their limited English, they always admonished their children — and later their grandchildren — to "Drink milk and study hard."

My parents lived a frugal and self-sustaining lifestyle. After work each day, Otoosan took a short coffee break and then tended to his garden and his banana patch. He and Okaasan grew nearly all the vegetables we ate. They also raised Easter lilies, ginger and other vegetables, which they sold to the plantation store.

Okaasan earned extra money by sewing *kappa* cloth raincoats for the Filipino sugar workers. During the war years, she took in the laundry of military personnel stationed near Kōloa. She did all of the laundry by hand, washing the clothes in a huge tub placed over an outdoor wood-burning stove. Using a stick, she pounded the water out of the garments. Some GIs brought Hershey bars and other goodies for us when they came to pick up their clean laundry. Okaasan continued to do the laundry in this manner until after the war.

Otoosan and Okaasan sacrificed for their children, seldom traveling to even the neighbor islands. Although they wanted to visit family and friends in Okinawa, they instead saved for our education. They made their first visit back to Okinawa in 1963, a year after I received my bachelor's degree.

As a family, we always supported each other. During my intermediate school years, my brother Robert and I worked on our cousin's hog farm on Saturdays and school vacation days. By my senior year in high school, I could take care of the hogs by myself when my cousin took time off from work. We gave all of the money we earned to our parents to help with the family's needs.

When all of us left for college on the Mainland, we knew we would not be able to return to Kaua'i until we received our degrees because we simply could not afford the expense. But a friendly football wager during my senior year earned me a free ticket home for Christmas — my first time home in over three years. Some of my high school classmates heard that I was coming home and greeted me at the Honolulu airport. One of them was Shirley Higashi, who would become my wife.

In 1980, I received my Master's degree in Educational Administration. It opened up new horizons for me, including the opportunity to serve as Provost of Kaua'i Community College from 1982 to 1997.

The Kaneshiro family, whose children Okaasan came to help care for, supported our family in so many ways. In her later years, it was those children — now adults — who looked out for Okaasan and our family.

One day, Okaasan came home from the bank, disappointed after being told she needed someone to co-sign a loan to help with her children's college expenses. Her nephew, Seiso Kaneshiro, told her that if she ever needed to borrow money, he would gladly help her — and he did.

After the war, Okaasan worked for her nephews, Seiko Kaneshiro and Mamoru Kaneshiro, who operated a peddling business. She also grew *moyashi* (bean sprouts) and made *konnyaku* to supplement the family income.

My parents sent us to college with the support of many people in our community. For example, Mr. Sasaki, who owned Sasaki Store, used to come to our house to take orders for canned goods. Okaasan usually served Mr. Sasaki tea and sweets. He always told her not to worry and just order what she needed. Years later, I learned that Mr. Sasaki had extended my parents about a thousand dollars worth of credit so that we wouldn't go hungry.

Okaasan paid off our debt to Mr. Sasaki by joining a *tanomoshi* group, which was like a money pot among friends or relatives who bid on the money. Okaasan always remembered Mr. Sasaki's kindness during those difficult years.

In 1990, while I was Provost of Kaua'i Community College, the school entered into an international exchange agreement with the University of the Ryukyus in

Okinawa. Over the next ten years, Kaua'i Community College hosted students from the University of the Ryukyus. One of the highlights of their visit to Kaua'i was spending an evening at my parents' home, where my mother shared with them her life experiences in Hawai'i. She talked about missing her home in Okinawa after having left at sixteen, and about wanting to return to Okinawa soon after arriving on Kaua'i. Okaasan told them about working in the sugar fields for ten cents an hour and she sang them this song, a combination of Japanese, Hawaiian and plantation pidgin.

> *Too muchee hanahana* (Too much work)
> *One dollar day* (For one dollar a day)
> *Yattemo yattemo* (No matter how hard I work)
> *Oro same pay.* (The pay is the same)

Okaasan described the working conditions on the plantations and told them about how the International Longshoremen's and Warehousemen's Union had organized strikes to help the workers get better wages and benefits. She told them about her life during the Depression years and expressed her gratitude to President Franklin Roosevelt for creating the Social Security system, which provided her an income in her retirement, and she said she was grateful that she had Medicare.

Okaasan visited Okinawa for the last time in 1995 at the age of 93. One of the highlights of her trip was a visit to the University of the Ryukyus, where she attended a dinner hosted by its President.

In August of 2002, Okaasan shared her stories with a group of high school teachers from Okinawa for the last time. She passed away about a month and a half later, just three months shy of her one-hundredth birthday.

Okaasan saw so many changes in her lifetime. As a young woman of sixteen, she had walked from her home to the port in Okinawa, where, by herself, she boarded the ship that brought her to Hawai'i. When she visited her native homeland for the first time in over four decades, she and Otoosan were driven to the airport, where they boarded an airplane that flew them to Okinawa. A journey that had taken weeks in 1919 was over in a matter of hours. In the early days of Okaasan's life in Hawai'i, her letters home had taken weeks to reach Okinawa. Later in her life, she could pick up the telephone and call her relatives in Okinawa and talk with them instantly. In spite of all the modern advances

Okaasan enjoyed, what she considered her greatest accomplishment was having given her children an education.

Even with her limited English-speaking abilities, she welcomed many university presidents — American and Okinawan — into her home and enjoyed conversing with them, because she wholeheartedly believed in the value of higher education.

I am grateful that my parents valued education and sacrificed in so many ways to give us, their children, a good education. And, I'm grateful to my brothers and sisters and our extended 'ohana, the Kaneshiros, and my wife Shirley and our two sons for supporting my educational pursuits and the rewarding career I enjoyed. We were all blessed to have grown up in beautiful Hawai'i, surrounded by people with so much *aloha* in their hearts.

Okagesama de…I am what I am thanks to all of you.

Yoshimitsu David Iha served the University of Hawai'i for more than forty years, including fifteen as Provost of Kaua'i Community College and nine as Secretary to the Board of Regents. Iha oversaw the development of Kaua'i Community College's Puhi campus from inception to completion. He also saw the college through two of Hawai'i's most destructive hurricanes, 'Iwa in 1982 and 'Iniki in 1992. As Provost, Iha was a strong advocate for international education, establishing exchange programs with educational institutions in Okinawa, Japan.

Iha has received numerous honors, among them the UH Alumni Association's Distinguished Service Award in 1988 and, in 2007, the Willard Wilson Award for Distinguished Service to the University of Hawai'i. In 2003, the University of the Ryukyus in Okinawa awarded Iha an Honorary Doctor of Philosophy degree.

Iha is a longtime practitioner of Urasenke tea ceremony. Since 1987, he has served as President of the Chado Urasenke Foundation Tankokai Kaua'i Association, which celebrated its twenty-fifth anniversary in July 2013. After retiring from UH, Iha began taking Okinawan *sanshin* lessons with the Afuso Ryu Gensei Kai Hawaii Shibu and has performed with his fellow students at *bon* dances around Kaua'i. Iha and his wife Shirley reside in Līhu'e and are the parents of two adult sons.

THERE IS ONLY GRATITUDE

Yoshiaki Fujitani

Having just celebrated my eighty-eighth, or *beiju*, birthday, an auspicious birthday in Japanese culture, in 2011, I look back with nostalgia on an eventful life lived fully in an exciting period in history. I would say that there is only gratitude for all the contributions people have made to my life.

I was born in a small, sleepy village nestled on the northern slopes of majestic Haleakalā on the island of Maui. Paʻuwela was the name of that village, but not many people knew of its existence until very recently when it gained notoriety as the location of "Banana Patch," the home of a hippie colony.

Father was the resident minister at Pauwela Hongwanji, a Buddhist temple comprised of people living within a radius of several miles, mainly in the towns of Haʻikū, Kuiaha and Paʻuwela, but others scattered further out as well — Peʻahi, Māliko and Kailua. Paʻuwela was the site of Haʻikū School, which was located just across the road from the temple. Father was appointed minister of the temple in 1921, as soon as he arrived from Japan, and served until 1934, when he was assigned to Moiliili Hongwanji in Honolulu. I was born in 1923, the second child and first son of Kodo and Aiko (Furukawa) Fujitani. This is the story of my life, which began in Paʻuwela.

It is recorded that the Japanese language school system in Hawaiʻi was started in 1907 when Bishop Yemyo Imamura, the second superintendent (*kantoku*) of the Honpa Hongwanji Mission of Hawaii, realized that the public schools provided good intellectual education for the youngster, but nothing in the way of moral training. It might be said, therefore, that Japanese language schools were started to provide education in traditional Japanese values rather than in language skills, although language was part of the curriculum. The particular course that took up values was known as *shūshin,* or "moral training," (literally, "to arrange or correct the inner self") and we learned such values as duty, justice, loyalty, courage, patience, effort, filial piety, responsibility, etc. Buddhists also offered *shi-on,* or the Four Gratitudes or Obligations — gratitude to parents, to one's country, to all beings and to the Buddha.

From very early then, the Japanese child was exposed to desirable values, which, it might be said, were made quite evident in the *Nisei* in war and peace. It is not unusual that that sense of gratitude remained with a person throughout his or her life. When in the early 1960s Bishop Shojitsu Ohara of the Hongwanji wrote, "Only when I have time I look at the mountain, but even when I'm occupied, the mountain is always looking at me," gratitude to the Most Compassionate Other — the Buddha — was evoked in me.

The list of people to whom I am indebted for my rich life begins before my birth and follows me to this day. They include my parents and babysitters, neighbors, teachers, fellow students, friends and comrades in the Military Intelligence Service, as well as fellow clergy.

There was an older man, Mr. Sugimoto, who lived with us in Paʻuwela, but separately in the temple basement, from whom I learned an early lesson. He was our yardman, gardener and handyman. One day — I must have been ten years old at the time — I asked him, "*Oji-chan,* what are you doing?" He replied, "Well, I'm shoring up the vegetable bed. If you don't keep on shoring it up, then it's going to flatten out and you won't have a vegetable bed. So, that's what we have to do — keep on shoring up the vegetable bed all the time."

I didn't understand his message until much later. He was saying that you cannot do something and feel that you've done everything and so you stop doing it. Shoring up a vegetable bed is a necessity, and that has to be done all the time. That kind of lesson stuck with me. But that simple lesson had lasting meaning for me in the years ahead, even to this day, reminding me constantly that there have been and are many hands shoring up the garden bed, which is me, to ensure a healthy physical, mental and spiritual life.

My idyllic life in Paʻuwela ended in the fall of 1934, when Father was assigned to Moiliili Hongwanji in Honolulu. Honolulu was quite different. Since I was a seventh grader, I enrolled at Washington Intermediate School. I suppose I looked like a country bumpkin, for, almost immediately, a student hijacked me of my lunch money.

After Washington, I went on to McKinley High School, where noted educator Dr. Miles E. Cary was principal. His advocacy of participatory democracy is well-known and I'm sure I was influenced a lot by that philosophy. But there were other teachers whom I remember fondly, such as Mrs. Ruth Gantt, Mrs. E. Logan-Smith, Mr. Archie Jackson and Mrs. Helen Griggs.

There was also Mrs. Ethel Spaulding, whose English class I took to make up a credit deficiency in order to graduate. Of course, she had no way of knowing that I would eventually become a minister, but the specific advice she gave me turned out to be prophetic. She said, "Yoshiaki, use your voice." Ever since, I have felt that in a speech, while the content is, of course, very important, the delivery, the enunciation, the proper emphasis, and one's voice are all equally vital in a successful and effective talk. Another unforgettable lesson was the "three ups and one down." If you have something to say, you get up, speak up, shut up and sit down. In other words, if you have something to say, say it, but be concise. Three ups and one down.

While at McKinley, it was in the Reserve Officers' Training Corps (ROTC) program and from my friends that I learned another lesson. I learned that a personal accomplishment is not a simple occurrence, but one that involves many elements. Firstly, there must be some form of impetus — a desire, a strong wish or will to do it. Then, there must be the ability, including the necessary skills, to do it. And, thirdly, there must be the opportunity to do it. If any of these elements are missing, there will be no accomplishment. The following event during my senior year illustrates the happy merging of the three elements.

There was a Junior ROTC program at McKinley that offered an annual drill team competition. Cadet officers ranked captain or higher were given the opportunity to organize and train a drill team. My friend, Cadet Captain Caesar Tsutsumi, had a truly "crack squad" that was the envy of the entire program. I wanted to have a team, too, but being only a second lieutenant, I was not qualified to have one. Caesar commanded his squad with great skill and I often stayed after school to watch him take the squad through its paces. One day, a few days before the competition, Caesar sought me out and to my surprise, asked me if I would take his place and command his squad in the competition. Of course, I was elated at the chance that I had been given and performed as well as I could and was rewarded with a first-place win. It was the opportunity that made the accomplishment possible, but my interest and desire to participate and the preparation that went into the competition were also necessary. Of course, it was a happy achievement for me, but anyone could see that I was simply riding on the accomplishments of my friend Caesar. The lesson I gained from that experience was that I should be prepared to handle the situation if the opportunity comes my way.

After graduating from McKinley, I went on to the University of Hawai'i, where I was a sophomore when Pearl Harbor was attacked on December 7, 1941. For a moment, we thought it was an elaborate maneuver being staged by the Navy, but soon came to the realization that the attack was real and, heeding the radio call for UH ROTC students to report to school, I walked up University Avenue and reported for duty. The UH ROTC was soon converted into the Hawai'i Territorial Guard (HTG) and organized. I was given the rank of corporal as one of the squad leaders in Company B. The commanding officer was Captain Nolle Smith, a highly respected athlete at the University. Our "top sergeant" was Ted Tsukiyama, a serious, no-nonsense twenty-year-old. The HTG unit filled in wherever they were needed in the defense of O'ahu, mostly doing guard duty. We served for a month and a half, guarding the piers, water tanks and other important facilities, until some bigwig in Washington decided that having a band of untrained youngsters who looked very much like the enemy was not the wisest decision. Of course, we were not heavily armed. We had five rounds of ammo only when we were standing guard. When our replacements came, we passed the five rounds over to them.

Late at night on January 19, Company B was assembled in the University gym and told by a teary-eyed Captain Smith that the services of those of Japanese ancestry were no longer needed. Although we were discharged from the HTG, the feeling among some of the students was that there must be something else that we could do. Soon, the 34th Engineers Auxiliary was organized when General Delos Emmons, commanding general of the Hawaiian Department in the days after Japan's attack on Pearl Harbor, accepted the plea of one hundred sixty-nine students who signed a petition to have the military use them as needed. The volunteers adopted the nickname, Varsity Victory Volunteers, and contributed to the war effort by building barracks, roads and laboring in the stone quarry, which helped, according to some historians, in the segregated 442nd Regimental Combat Team being authorized in 1943.

While the HTG was in existence, there was a story being circulated, though perhaps apocryphal. I like to tell it because our squad was operating in the vicinity of the story. Our squad was billeted in the Dillingham Building on the lower end of Bishop Street and our assignment was to guard the pier area. According to the story, a few days after the war started, a troopship full of Marines entered Honolulu Harbor and docked at Pier 8. The Marines eagerly converged on the bow of the ship and saw, to their surprise, a squad of HTG men (us) dressed in World War I garb, leggings, flat helmets and armed with World War I rifles (Springfield '03 five rounds bolt action pieces) with shiny chrome-plated parade bayonets attached, pacing the pier. Then, it is said, a horrified Marine, nudging his neighbor, whispered, "Hey, Mac, we're too late."

Although I volunteered for the Triple V and went to Schofield Barracks, I didn't remain there for very long, because in April of 1942, my father was arrested and incarcerated on the Mainland as a "potentially dangerous enemy alien," so I had to return home to help with my family's finances. When the 442nd Regimental Combat Team was formed and thousands of our young men went to Camp Shelby, I was not ready to go. But when, in the latter part of 1943, a deputation team came from Minnesota to enlist linguists for the Military Intelligence Service, I was ready and was inducted into the Army in January of 1944. I was shipped to Minnesota just in time for the start of the February 1944 class of the Military Intelligence Service Language School (MISLS) at Camp Savage. I still remember my first view of the camp, beautifully clad in new fallen snow.

In May of that year, the school was moved to Fort Snelling on the outskirts of St. Paul and, taking advantage of summer break, I journeyed to Santa Fe, New Mexico, to visit Father who was incarcerated at a U.S. Department of Justice detention camp. Since I had not seen him for a couple of years, the reunion was emotional, but otherwise uneventful.

After nine months in a crash course in Japanese military language at Camp Savage, I was assigned to the Pacific Military Intelligence Research Section (PACMIRS) to do translation work.

When the war ended, our unit was sent to Tōkyō to collect documents of military value. In Tōkyō, I met my cousins, who went out of their way to make me welcome and, in January, I went to visit my grandmother — my mother's mother — in the village of Yatsuo in Tōyama Prefecture. These were happy moments, but there were a few disturbing incidents in Tōkyō. We were billeted in the NYK building, where the obviously malnourished young Japanese workers serving in the cafeteria would come unabashedly to beg for food. Once, I was approached on the street by a father who asked for whatever I could give him so that he could feed his children. The begging didn't bother me, since I understood the circumstances. What bothered me the most was that these suffering people, ostensibly our enemies, looked so much like me. I am an American, I affirmed, but I was also Japanese, I realized.

In late March, our unit headed back to Washington, D.C., to work on the documents we had collected in Tōkyō. We used to joke among ourselves about the "easy life" we had, as there was no morning drill or physical exercise requirement of any kind. You know the term "airborne outfit?" We used to call ourselves "chairborne." By the end of the year, after serving a few days short of three years, I was discharged from the Army.

In February 1947, I returned to the University of Hawai'i to complete the second semester of my sophomore year and began the process of enrolling at the University of Chicago, where I was accepted for the fall quarter with my schooling paid for courtesy of the GI Bill of Rights, which was the greatest reward for our service in the armed services of the United States. I spent five years at the University of Chicago, from 1947 to 1952, and received a Master of Arts degree in the Committee of History of Culture under the instruction of Dr. Joachim Wach, a noted Swiss-German scholar who had done some work in Buddhism.

By then, my resolve to work towards becoming a Buddhist minister had been made, not because I was that knowledgeable or that holy or spiritual. During my time away from Hawai'i, including the time spent in the Army, I began to feel that unless the *Nisei* came back to Hawai'i to continue in the spread of Buddhism, then Buddhism would disappear. So, I thought I have to learn Buddhism so that I can be of some help. It was not because I was spiritually prepared, but because I saw the need. And so, I applied to Kyōto University to study basic Buddhism with Dr. Gadjin Nagao, another noted scholar who was an authority, especially in Tibetan Buddhism. In Kyōto, I was able to study also with Dr. Toshio Ando, who specialized in Tendai Buddhism at Otani (Higashi Hongwanji) University, and with Professor Ryugyo Fujimoto and Professor Ryosetsu Fujiwara of Ryūkoku (Honpa Hongwanji) University. Both Professor Fujimoto and Professor Fujiwara helped to prepare me for my ordination in the Honpa Hongwanji clergy.

When I left Kyōto to return home to be assigned as a minister, Professor Nagao gave me some advice. He said, "When you go back to Hawai'i and work in your position as a minister, don't think in terms of teaching with great sermons. Real teaching has to come from your being, your lesson. You have to live your lesson, not just talk about it."

18

Ordained in 1956, I returned to Hawai'i and was immediately assigned to be assistant minister at Wailuku Hongwanji on Maui, where Father was the resident minister until 1958, when he retired. After serving for two years as resident minister, I was assigned to the main temple in Honolulu. Before leaving Wailuku, however, there was an event that proved to be very significant in my career as a Hongwanji minister.

It must have been in 1959 when Father Putman of Christ the King Catholic Church in Kahului entered our temple and offered incense, actually participating in a Buddhist funeral ceremony being held for the mother of one of his parishioners. Up to that very moment, it had been common knowledge that Catholics, by church law, were forbidden to set foot in a non-Catholic place of worship. The startling lesson I learned was that even people of different faiths can respect each other's beliefs and have an amicable relationship.

I took that lesson to Honolulu, where one of the earliest events I attended in the community was the first Union Thanksgiving Service, comprised of a group of interfaith clergy and held at the St. Clement's Episcopal Church on Wilder Avenue on Thanksgiving eve, 1960. The rector there was the Rev. Paul Wheeler. Included were clergy from the Unitarian Church, Jewish Temple, Methodist Church, Soto (Buddhist) Mission and the Catholic Church. An interesting aspect of that first gathering was that the Rev. Ernest Hunt, a Buddhist, who was to give the first interfaith Thanksgiving message, could not be present and so his message was read by Rev. Wheeler, an Episcopalian Christian. The tradition of this interfaith service has continued to the present, with the participating temples or churches taking turns in hosting. A unique consequence of that arrangement is that unprecedented things occur, as in my case, when I was the speaker when the service was held at Temple Emanu-El. There is no doubt that such a gathering has brought stability, respect and friendship to our community.

In 1975, I was elected the eleventh Bishop of the Honpa Hongwanji Mission of Hawaii, succeeding Rev. Kanmo Imamura, who retired before the end of his term when he reached the age of seventy. As his assistant, I served as the interim bishop from August 1974 until the election in February of the following year. I've always believed that this was my community, not so much in terms of ownership, but because I was born here and grew up here, and thus, even as a minister, I considered the whole community to be my field of operation. I hope it doesn't sound too ostentatious, but that's how I felt. It might have been simply a strong love of my hometown. I believe the Honpa Hongwanji Mission of Hawaii's adoption of the

19

"Living Treasures of Hawai'i" Program in 1976 was a direct fruit of that conviction. It is not a program to honor only Buddhists or Hongwanji members, but any individual who has contributed towards making Hawai'i a more humane society. Here again, is the expression of gratitude for the gifts that we are constantly receiving.

I was privileged to serve twelve years in the position of Bishop, from 1975 to 1987, but at age sixty-four, I felt I was too young to retire, so I accepted an appointment to the dual position of Director of Buddhist Education and Director of the Buddhist Study Center (BSC). After six years, from 1987 to 1993, I finally retired from the Hongwanji at age seventy. During those six years, there was a program at the BSC in which people from the community were invited to a monthly program titled, "Friendship Circle." In retrospect, it was an excellent opportunity for us to get to know the community and for our guests to get to know the Buddhist Study Center and the Buddhist community.

I retired for a second time in 2009 after ten years with the Bukkyo Dendo Kyokai (BDK) — the Society for the Promotion of Buddhism. The primary function of BDK was to distribute the book, "Teaching of Buddha," in hotel rooms in Hawai'i.

I'm fortunate that I have an active life and a loving family and that I have been surrounded all my life by wise and kind people who have instilled in me solid values, especially humility and gratitude, which helped me prepare myself for a meaningful existence.

Postscript: Although retired, Rev. Fujitani is often asked to deliver the invocation or benediction at memorial services for AJA (Americans of Japanese ancestry) veterans and, as a veteran himself, he says he is always happy and privileged to honor his brothers who served. Rev. Fujitani's always-thoughtful compositions for these occasions inspire reverence, remembrance and enlightenment. The following is an example of his offerings — this one shared at the Oahu AJA Veterans Council's Joint Memorial Service for World War II AJA veterans on September 30, 2007.

In this hallowed cemetery where our comrades now lie in silent repose, we come to remember these valiant men who fought in distant battlefields and gave their lives so that we may enjoy the fruits of freedom.

But we come, too, to reaffirm and thereby perpetuate the great values that sustained our nation in war and peace and engendered by this generation, so that future generations may also enjoy the benefits of a society solidly built on the foun-

dations of the values of respect and fairness, of honor and loyalty, of courage and forbearance, and perseverance, magnanimity and compassion.

We come also to voice our gratitude for this wondrous land we call our home and the beautiful golden people who inhabit these islands. We are indeed blessed.

May this moment of camaraderie, may the message of our distinguished speaker inspire us in the days ahead to strive for a life enriched by an awareness and appreciation of the myriad joys that surround us and thereby permit us to contribute towards a saner and happier world of which we would want to be integral parts.

Namu Amida Butsu. Homage to the Most Compassionate One...

Yoshiaki Fujitani has served on the boards of the Hawaii Association of International Buddhists, Samaritan Counseling Center of Hawaiʻi (since renamed the Counseling & Spiritual Care Center of Hawaiʻi), American Civil Liberties Union and the Military Intelligence Service Veterans Club.

Many young people consider Fujitani a mentor, among them Dr. David Coleman, Dean of Humanities and Fine Arts at Chaminade University of Honolulu. Coleman remembers meeting Fujitani for the first time in the mid-1980s at a conference on Buddhist-Christian dialogue at the University of California at Berkeley. The two spent the evening talking about the need for dialogue between religions and about the responsibility all people share in working for a more just and peaceful society.

"A brilliant mind and a humble leader, he became my mentor through the decades to follow. He would come to guest-lecture in my Buddhism classes and helped lead visits by my students to the temple. He was conversant in both traditions, a gentle teacher, and a quiet, but determined advocate for the poor and the rights of all people," Coleman shared.

In 2003, Chaminade University established the BDK Fujitani Interfaith Program, a lecture series focused on justice and peace that sought to foster understanding and dialogue between the Christian and Buddhist communities and the society at large. "He did not want us to name the program after him, but we convinced him that such an honor was in service to the goals we had set for the program," Coleman added.

Fujitani has been honored by numerous organizations, including the McKinley High School Alumni Association and the Honpa Hongwanji Mission of Hawaii, which recognized him as a "Living Treasure of Hawai'i" in 1994. In 2012, the University of Hawai'i at Mānoa Colleges of Arts and Sciences presented its "Serving Heart Award" to Fujitani in recognition of his "extraordinary" service to individuals and the community. Later that year, the Government of Japan recognized Fujitani's efforts to bridge Japan, Hawai'i and the United States by presenting him The Wooden Cup with the Chrysanthemum Crest. Fujitani and his wife Tomi are the parents of three adult children and six grandchildren.

"HOW" MATTERS

Herbert K. Shimabukuro

In my formative years, my father was my most influential teacher. I learned many things as I worked alongside him every day. But the most valuable lesson he imparted upon me was the importance of *yarikata* — the way one does things.

As we worked together on our hog farm in Kalihi Valley and he explained what needed to be done, he would always remind me, "*Yarikata wa daiji,*" meaning the way you do things is important. If I did it right the first time, I wouldn't have to go back and *yarinaosu* — re-do, or fix — what had already been done.

Years later in law school, I failed to connect that important lesson with my legal studies.

I attended George Washington University Law School in Washington, D.C., from August 1954 to June 1957. It was a great learning experience in every respect.

One of the required courses during my first semester was titled "Contracts." I was genuinely interested in the subject and studied earnestly and diligently. My professor, Charles Bouvier, was an excellent teacher. Knowing that we were all new to the study of law, he suggested that we take a practice exam a few weeks before the actual written examination. In law school, all of our examinations were written essays that were given only once, at the end of the semester. There were no six-week exams or monthly quizzes or tests. That one written exam not only determined whether the student passed or failed the class, but his or her grade for the course. All of us first-year law students were, understandably, apprehensive about the weight the single examination carried.

To allay our anxiety, Professor Bouvier suggested the practice exam, much to our relief.

A few days later, Professor Bouvier returned our graded practice exams. I was shocked when I received my test paper. Written at the top of the first page was a big "F." In all my years in school, I had never received an "F."

Professor Bouvier used the remainder of the class time to review the material that had been covered in the practice exam. As I listened to his review, I felt confident that I understood the material and had presented it clearly and accurately in my practice exam.

Although I normally would not question my professor's judgment, in this case, I was confident that I had answered the exam questions correctly, so I decided to ask him why he had given me an "F."

I told Professor Bouvier that my answers to the exam questions were consistent with his summary. He looked me straight in the eye and said, "I didn't read your paper because it was illegible. I couldn't read your handwriting." I was so ashamed. But he was right.

"I'm sorry, Professor," I told him.

I learned a valuable lesson from Professor Bouvier — and that was the importance of writing clearly and legibly so that people can read and understand what I have written. That is what it means to respect the person to whom you are presenting your written material. I later realized that with the pressure and anxiety of taking my first law school examination, albeit a practice exam, I had forgotten what my father had imparted upon me about *yarikata*. How a person writes — his or her penmanship — is as important as knowing the subject matter. When the "real" examination on contracts was given later in the semester, I wrote as clearly and as legibly as I could. Professor Bouvier gave me an "A" for the course.

Thereafter, and throughout law school, the bar examinations and, subsequently, whenever I wrote for others, I always tried my best to write as clearly as I possibly could.

Yarikata would continue to guide my work in the practice of law. I believe it was instrumental in the State of Hawai'i Judicial Selection Commission's decision to submit my name for a judgeship to then-Chief Justice of the Hawai'i Supreme Court, Herman Lum. In February of 1986, Chief Justice Lum appointed me to a District Court judgeship in the First Circuit. At the time, he told me that he liked the way I had handled a case that had come before the Judiciary nine years earlier.

I am eternally grateful to my father for teaching me about *yarikata* all those many years ago — and to Professor Bouvier for reminding me that how one writes, or does anything — *yarikata* — is important.

After retiring as a State Circuit Court judge in 1998, I served as President of the Haneji Club, my family's Okinawan locality club, from 2002 to 2010. The club was formed as a mutual assistance organization in 1928 by the *Issei* who had immigrated to the Hawaiian Islands from the village of Haneji in Okinawa, Japan. Another mission of the Haneji Club is to promote friendship and harmony and, like our *Issei* founders, to support our members in their times of need. We have an annual New Year's party and a picnic, and every year, we participate in the Hawaii United Okinawa Association's (HUOA) Okinawan Festival at Kapiʻolani Park and its craft fairs. My wife Lillian and our sons have supported me in all of my club and HUOA activities.

The Haneji Club is one of the member-clubs of the HUOA, whose mission is to preserve, promote and perpetuate the Okinawan/Japanese culture. Implicit in this mission is the preservation and perpetuation of the values learned from our *Issei* parents — values such as *shinbō* (patience), *doryoku* (effort), *on* (obligation), *kansha* (gratitude), *okagesama de* (because of your support), *oyakōkō* (love your parents), *ganbare* (persevere), *gaman* (tolerance), *kyōryoku* (cooperation) and *wa* (harmony and peace). These cultural values were instilled in me by my *Issei* parents, who were educated in Japanese schools in Okinawa, and were the same values my parents had learned from their parents. It is these values that sustain me today, two generations later, and the values that my wife and I tried to instill in our sons as they were growing up.

My father used to say that *gakumon* (education) was important, but that in order to be a good person, "*chi mo namida mo aru hito*" — one had to have "blood and tears." In other words, a good person must have feelings and compassion.

As the Dalai Lama has written, human beings should have empathy and compassion. He said that kindness is one of the best human values and that kindness and respect for others and one's self will help to bring about a just, harmonious and peaceful world.

It is my hope that our descendants and future generations will hold fast to those timeless values that have sustained us through the years and that they will continue to strive to make the world a place of peace and harmony.

~

Herbert K. Shimabukuro enjoyed a full and rewarding career as a lawyer and jurist. Early in his career, he joined the Honolulu Japanese Chamber of Commerce and served as its President in 1966.

In 2000, Shimabukuro was asked to serve on the State of Hawai'i's Judicial Evaluation Review Panel. Since retiring in 1998, Shimabukuro has devoted much of his time to the Hawaii United Okinawa Association (HUOA) on activities related to his Okinawan heritage. He enjoys helping with the annual Okinawan Festival and the HUOA's various fund-raising craft fairs. On occasion, he is asked to install the HUOA's incoming officers. In 1987, and again from 2002 to 2010, Shimabukuro served as President of Haneji Club, which is made up of descendants of immigrants from Haneji-*son* (village) in Okinawa. For over twenty years, he and his wife Lillian have provided "water boy" duties, supporting Haneji Club's softball team by serving the players snacks and refreshments. The Shimabukuros are the parents of three adult sons.

THE LIFE-CHANGING JOURNEY

George Suzuki

My childhood and early teen years were spent on 'Ewa Plantation. It was the 1930s. I remember the sugar plantation workers toiling in the fields across from our house. These memories remained with me all my life and profoundly influenced my thinking.

The *Issei* — the first-generation immigrants from Japan — passed on to their *Nisei* children, my generation, the values that had been ingrained in them while growing up in Japan. One of the most important of these values was *on*. It is a Japanese word that is hard to define in English, but it refers to an obligation that is owed to someone, or a debt of gratitude in the deepest sense. This value was one of the first that Japanese children learned — to be deeply grateful to the land of their birth, which gave them life and sustenance. Along with gratitude came an obligation to serve.

I remember a fellow *Nisei* telling me about his *Issei* mother's words just before she returned to Japan prior to the outbreak of World War II. She foresaw war between our two countries on the horizon. "War is about to start," she told her son. "I am going back to my country, Japan. You must stay and fight for your country, America."

At home, I spoke only English, so I was considerably handicapped in speaking and writing Japanese when I started first grade of Japanese language school. Although I managed to understand the sound of some words and phrases, I continued to have a hard time grasping the language and finally dropped out in the fourth grade. Still, I have fond memories of Japanese school and am forever grateful to my *sensei* (teacher), who gave up her precious time to tutor me so that I could catch up with the rest of the class.

I enjoyed lining up in front of the school, where we exercised, bowed and paid our respects to the principal and teachers. I admired our principal, who was a straight and upright man with a small mustache. He was firm with the students, but we all knew that he cared for us.

My favorite subject in Japanese school was *shūshin*. I grew to admire Ninomiya Kinjiro, the boy in Japan who read books while carrying firewood on his back, and I was inspired by the story of the mother who urged her son with the injured hand to become a doctor.

I was in high school during most of the World War II years. I used to ride the bus to and from my school, which was located in town. Every school day, the bus would pass Pearl Harbor, where I saw the row of sunken American battleships in the water next to Ford Island. Commuting to school on the bus gave me the opportunity to observe the Pacific War from the perspective of Oʻahu, which was the main staging area for the battles that were raging in the western Pacific at the time. The war was going badly for Japan.

The bus I rode to school was usually full of young servicemen. The entire military and civilian population of Oʻahu seemed to pass through the Oahu Railway bus terminal in Iwilei, which was always packed with thousands of servicemen on leave. They had cash in their pockets and time on their hands. Some of those servicemen would soon be departing to enter battle.

Despite my Japanese face, I never encountered any hostile or threatening remarks. In fact, many of the servicemen who sat next to me on the bus were friendly and curious about the textbooks I was reading. Some of them were just out of high school themselves and wanted to know about my high school courses.

My father had been a U.S. Army reservist in World War I, so he befriended some of the servicemen who were stationed near our house and invited them over. I still keep in touch with a few of them.

On August 6, 1945, the United States dropped an atomic bomb on Hiroshima, Japan. At the time, news of the bombing had little impact on me; I didn't even know what an atomic bomb was, and I knew only vaguely where Hiroshima was located. The war ended three days later when a second atomic bomb was dropped on Nagasaki City.

In 1945, I entered the University of Hawaiʻi. Before I could even start my second semester, I was drafted into the U.S. Army. I was assigned to the Medical Corps at Tripler General Hospital at Fort Shafter after basic training and was discharged a year later. I returned to classes at the University of Hawaiʻi, and since I was considered a World War II veteran, I received all of the educational benefits afforded veterans by the GI Bill of Rights.

I decided to transfer to the University of Michigan as an undergraduate pre-medical student. Being admitted to the University of Michigan Medical School was a major milestone in my life.

After graduating from medical school in 1953, I interned at the Henry Ford Hospital in Detroit, Michigan. I remember thinking that working as a medical intern was as grueling as working in the cane fields of ʻEwa, only the hours in the hospital were longer.

Midway through my internship, I developed a serious case of infectious mononucleosis and was hospitalized for three weeks. Although I recovered and was able to complete my internship, I had to put off what would be a strenuous postgraduate training schedule because the mononucleosis had left me chronically fatigued.

While hospitalized, I had read a medical journal article about a facility in Hiroshima called the Atomic Bomb Casualty Commission. It was operated jointly by the U.S. and Japan governments and was designed to study the effects of the atomic bomb on its human survivors. At the time, I was just beginning to develop an interest in Japan and its people and, Hiroshima, to me, was a place where an atomic bomb had been dropped and thousands of people had lost their lives.

I completed my internship and applied for a job with the National Academy of Sciences in Washington, D.C. My contract with the Atomic Bomb Casualty Commission in Hiroshima was for two years. After my academic credentials had been reviewed and I had obtained my security clearance and was interviewed in Washington, D.C., I was accepted for the job.

I still remember my arrival in Hiroshima. I thought I had stepped onto a different planet. Most of the rubble from the atomic bombing had been cleared, but the city looked like a Third World country. The people were impoverished and many were in need of jobs, shelter and better nutrition. I began my work as a physician, examining atomic bomb survivors of every description.

I knew that many Hawaiʻi AJAs (Americans of Japanese ancestry) were descendants of immigrants who had come from Hiroshima Prefecture. In fact, many of the words spoken by Hawaiʻi Japanese were rooted in the Hiroshima dialect.

After having spent seven years studying medicine in the United States, I could see the differences between Japanese and American culture. Americans were direct, frank and practical, while Japanese people tended to be indirect, polite and deferential.

Despite the depressed economic conditions, the Japanese always went out of their way to include a bit of art in every aspect of their lives, be it with a flower arrangement or a hanging scroll, even in the humblest of homes. Morning glories were planted in pots to brighten up the drabness of wooden houses that stood along the road. Even taxicab drivers decorated their cars with tiny pots of fresh flowers for their passengers.

In Hiroshima, the custom of *okaeshi* — of returning a gift or favor — was taken very seriously. If you gave someone a gift or did him or her a favor, something equivalent or better would be returned to you in a few days. Interestingly, this custom or value is still practiced among Japanese Americans in Hawai'i.

Witnessing these acts of kindness amidst the destruction and suffering reminded me of something my mother had told my siblings and me when we were growing up. She said that Japan was a great country (*"Nihon wa erai kuni desu"*), and she taught us to be proud of our Japanese heritage.

My friendships with the doctors in Hiroshima would last a lifetime. Many of the Hiroshima doctors, some of whom had survived the atomic bombing, were eager to learn English from me. They were happy that I spoke with them only in English and that I corrected their pronunciation and grammar until I was satisfied that they had grasped it. The doctors hoped to further their medical knowledge and training in the United States, which had been suspended due to the war.

When my two-year contract was up, I left Hiroshima and began my internal medicine residency in San Francisco. After completing four years of training, I opened my office in Honolulu. To my great pleasure and surprise, some of the people I had seen working in the sugarcane fields in 'Ewa became my first patients. Because I had learned to speak Japanese during my time in Hiroshima, my practice flourished, as many of my patients felt comfortable speaking to me in Japanese.

When I began my practice, I vowed to adhere to certain principles: to listen carefully to each patient, and after performing examinations and tests, I would explain my findings and treatment plan to my patient in detail. I vowed to base medical treatments and procedures on solid scientific evidence and studies, and as much as possible, I tried to keep the number of medications and procedures to a minimum so as to avoid side effects and drug interactions. I tried to follow the Hippocratic Oath, "…above all, do no harm."

My decision to go to Hiroshima at the beginning of my medical career impacted my life and my practice of medicine profoundly.

I was privileged to have been able to serve as a doctor in Hawai'i for forty-five years. I've had the good fortune of living my life in a community where the many ethnic groups live and work together in harmony. Perhaps this is because many of Hawai'i's young people have in their genetic makeup the many races that live in Hawai'i.

My life has spanned the Great Depression and the sugar plantation era of Hawai'i, six major wars and the Hawai'i of the present. Today's Hawai'i is a vastly improved society and we look forward to an even brighter future.

George Suzuki maintained his friendship with the doctors and other medical personnel he met during his time in Hiroshima and continued to work with doctors who visited Hawai'i to examine atomic bomb survivors who had settled in the Islands. Suzuki retired in 2008 after forty-five years as a practicing physician. In his retirement, he pursued his interest in various subjects, including history, and was a member of the Hawaii Hiroshima Heritage Study Group. In 2005, Suzuki was presented The Order of the Rising Sun, Gold and Silver Rays, by the Government of Japan for his efforts at forging goodwill between the United States and Japan. He and his wife Esther raised four adult children. Suzuki died in August 2011.

LEARNING TO WALK
IN THE SHOES OF OTHERS

James T. Tanabe

After I received my Bachelor's degree from the University of Hawai'i, and then my Master's in Social Work from the University of Chicago, my father, Kintoku Tanabe, imparted some wisdom that remained with me throughout my professional life and even after I retired.

Papa was an *Issei* — a first-generation immigrant from Japan. Although he was not a highly educated man, he reminded me that my education and the degrees I had earned would be meaningless and of no help to me in my professional life unless I could communicate with common people. So, to Papa goes the credit for the success I enjoyed when I applied his advice in my work with troubled youth and families. He was able to give me this valuable advice because he understood it firsthand.

My father came to Hawai'i from Hiroshima, Japan, in the early 1900s and labored on the sugar plantations for four years, from 1906 until 1910. At night, he learned to read and speak English — this, after a hard day of work in the fields. Learning English helped Papa advance from the fields to the office, where he became a plantation bookkeeper. He then took a job as a stock boy and sales clerk at City Mill, a building materials supplier. Papa then took all of his past work experiences and became a traveling hardware salesman for Theo H. Davies on the Big Island. It was then that he married my mother, who was from his hometown in Hiroshima.

Papa traveled all over the Big Island, selling his wares to customers out of a horse and buggy rig, until the company provided him with an automobile. In 1928, Papa started his own furniture business in Honolulu.

From his experiences, I learned that life is an accumulation of knowledge gained from past experiences. You use those experiences and lessons to propel yourself forward, to the next phase of your life.

In my life, I have come to realize that the Japanese word, *oyakōkō*, which is defined as filial piety, or caring for your parents, isn't just about looking after one's parents or doing things for them. It means honoring your parents, grandparents and elders by truly listening to them and seeking their guidance because you respect their life experiences and their teachings.

I was a rebellious child while growing up. I wanted to be independent from my parents. Ironically, as I grew older, I realized that so many of the successes I enjoyed in my professional life were the result of taking to heart my father's advice and teachings. Papa was teaching me to do my work with humility.

I completed my graduate studies in social work in the summer of 1968. My employer, the Cook County Juvenile Court of Chicago, Illinois, paid my tuition to graduate school. I was a Korean War veteran, so the GI Bill supplemented my trainee's salary during my two years in school.

After receiving my Master's degree from the University of Chicago School of Social Work, I was immediately appointed the supervisor of a unit consisting of six probation officers. There were forty such units. I was the only person of Asian ancestry and the only one from Hawai'i to be hired as a supervisor. In my job interview, the chief probation officer asked me why I thought I was qualified to be a probation officer for juvenile delinquents. I explained that I had been rebellious while growing up and had had my share of trouble with authority figures. Because of that, I felt I understood juvenile delinquents and could help them.

I had grown up in the Sheridan-Pāwa'a district of Honolulu. When I was ten years old, we moved to the Liliha-Pu'unui area of town. I began my high school years at 'Iolani School, which is a private school. However, because I encountered behavior problems involving fighting, I transferred to McKinley High School, a public school.

As I did my work as a social worker, I often reflected on Papa's advice while working with my staff.

One of the requirements I made for myself as a supervisor was to get out from behind my desk and accompany my probation officers on home visits and school visitations; I also assigned myself some cases. As their supervisor, it was within my scope of responsibilities to institute changes like this. My administrator supported me because it helped all of us to better understand what our clients were facing so that we could better serve them.

On home visits, I saw with my own eyes how the people lived and communicated. Most of these families lived in poverty and were not well educated. Whenever I was offered coffee or something to eat — even if I had seen roaches running around in the house, or unsanitary living conditions — I thought back to what Papa had told me and I accepted whatever was offered to me. By simply sharing a cup of coffee with the families, they came to trust me and confide in me. I made them feel comfortable with me, which enabled me to get the information I needed to prepare more insightful reports. I showed my clients that I could be stern, yet empathetic in handling their situation.

One of my responsibilities was to write reports, which the judges referred to in deciding on treatment for the juveniles who came before their court. I applied the same philosophy when working with kids — I communicated with them on their level. One day, I stopped one of the case attorneys in the hallway and told him, "I'm going to make you a promise: The day I stop getting mad at these kids, I'm gonna quit." I continued to work in juvenile justice for some thirty-five years, despite it being a field notorious for its high staff turnover.

When I was angry with the kids, I told them so with compassion, because I wanted them to be good and to have a good future. It was just as my father had done for me. My admonitions were stern, as Papa's had been, but I realized that he told me those things because he cared about me.

I owe whatever successes I may have had in my career to my father's admonition to not think too highly of myself and what I had accomplished, but rather to always try to connect with people, heart to heart, no matter what their station in life may be.

James T. Tanabe and his wife Yoshie returned to Hawai'i in 1992 after twenty-five years in Chicago. During a visit to the USS Arizona Memorial, they viewed a film that pointed to Hawai'i's Japanese Americans as having assisted in Japan's bombing of Pearl Harbor in December 1941. The Tanabes protested the film's allegation and were successful in having it deleted. The Tanabes are active members of the Japanese American Citizens League-Honolulu Chapter.

A Korean War veteran, Tanabe is also an active member of the MIS Veterans Club of Hawaii and was its newsletter editor for many years.

In 2008, the Hawaii Pacific Gerontological Society presented Tanabe its Na Lima Kokua Award for his community service. The award recognized him for conducting oral histories of World War II Military Intelligence Service veterans and those who served with the occupation forces in Japan.

BECOMING "JAPANESE"

Lionel Yukio Tokioka

(From a September 2012 interview by Fujio Matsuda and Drusilla Tanaka)

Lionel Tokioka is the first son of Masayuki and Harue Tokioka, both of whom had immigrated to Hawai'i from Japan. In the local Japanese community, which was made up largely of Buddhists, the Tokiokas were an anomaly: They were Christians.

When it was time for Lionel to attend school, his parents enrolled him in Punahou School, which was founded by Christian missionaries and where Lionel was one of the few nonwhite children. He recalled his first day of school in September 1941 and the less-than-welcoming-reception he received.

"First thing that happened to me…my mother dropped me off and told me, 'You go up the stairs and they'll tell you what class to go to.' So that's what I do.

They ask me, 'Hey, what's your name?'

'Yukio.'

'What's your last name?'

I just shake my head — no one told me what my last name is. So, I repeat the only name I know: 'Yukio.'

They look all over the list and no 'Yukio.' So everybody goes to class, except me. And, finally, they were concerned and asked, 'What is your name, again?'

'Yukio.'

'Is your name Lionel?' I shake my head.

'Tokioka?' Again, shake my head.

Well, they finally figure it out — hey, he's the only one left, so must be him. So that's the beginning of all the discrimination that I've had. So, I stand out."

On December 7, 1941, Lionel learned for the first time that he was Japanese. A caring neighbor warned him that his playmates at school might not be very nice to him. His neighbor's warning did not adequately prepare him for the reality of the cruel treatment he and other children of Japanese ancestry received at school. His father explained to Lionel that there are good people and there are bad people, but most are good people who will help him cope.

Although his friends teased him about being "born with a silver spoon in his mouth," while in the Army, he realized that his family's wealth could not help him as an enlisted man. He learned to be patient in striving to achieve his personal objectives and also learned how to navigate the system. In doing so, Lionel was able to help others through the system. In his words:

"When you are a [rank of] private, it's not much fun. But, if you know all of the regulations, guess what? They can't push you around. There are some rules and regs that they have to follow, too. That's why I was the 'guardhouse lawyer.'"

After completing his military service, Lionel attended graduate school. He then returned to Hawai'i to work for his father's company.

"One of the first things that I did was to find out that, again, I went to Punahou; I went to college; I know nobody in Hawai'i, I mean, very few [people]. And, so, I'm starting work over here at National Mortgage, so I figured I got to get

to know people. So then I was invited to join the [Honolulu] Japanese Junior Chamber of Commerce. And, now, all of a sudden, I get involved. And who do I get involved with over there? Masa Kamisato. So, he was the President and he was doing all these things. And I asked him, 'How can you do all these things?' He explained to me all the things that he does, taught me a lot. One of the things he taught me, he said, 'One thing you gotta know is Robert's Rules of Order. You can run a meeting. If you know the stuff, you can control the meeting.' And, so, knowing these things, pretty soon, I've never been intimidated. I know all of this stuff, and it's dangerous when I get it. But, again, that's the Chamber — taught me all of that. And, I met people and some who became politicians. That's how I learned politics."

Eventually, though, Lionel learned that control over a situation can be lost. He related his disappointment over the sale of International Savings & Loan to City Bank, which eventually merged with Central Pacific Bank.

"I think that if I had stayed there [with City Bank, if] our group stayed in, we would have done better than what Central Pacific has done. But that's not what happened. In the process, people made a lot of money. I didn't, in comparison to others, and I didn't need it, but a lot of our people could have done better. They got compensated in monetary ways, but as far as being able to do things, I don't think so. [It's important] to have a say as to what happens, the other way…and again, one of these things is learning values. You find out that, you know what, hey, money isn't everything. Unfortunately, everybody has a different perspective. To some people, I think the money was more important."

While Lionel was moving up the corporate ladder prior to the sale of International Savings & Loan, he said he felt a "reverse discrimination" of sorts from his colleagues when he became the bank's President. However, he focused on running a good company and revealed his goal to the *dōjō* Zen master, Rotaishi Tanoue.

"He asked me, 'What are you trying to do with your company?' After talking to him, I told him, 'I want to bring some of our staff people up here to listen, and if you could give them some philosophical understandings so that we can

know what it is when we're doing business, how we should do business...' He said, 'Yeah, great. We can do that.' Then he asked me, 'What are you trying to do?' So, I said, 'I'd like to...' What I was trying to do was to create a company that would be an example of how companies should be run so that it can be taught throughout the world. In the end, it came down to, I don't know if I can make a dent into anything. I just hope I can be the start. So, I tried with International [Savings & Loan]. If you go back and talk to the people that worked with me and talk about the good ol' days — we had a good company, and I think all companies could be like that. I don't know if I was able to influence anyone, but if I did, that would be my greatest satisfaction. One of the big satisfactions I do get is when these guys see me on the street — and some of them I remember and some I don't — but, invariably, they say, 'You know what, that was the best time' that they had in their lives as far as working. And I get a great deal of satisfaction out of that."

From an early age, Lionel learned to respect his elders.

"I tend to give credit to my father all the time, but actually, this is all communicated to me by my mother. My mother interprets, and my father just sits there. 'Your father doesn't like you to do this. You shouldn't be doing this, or you should be doing this, or you should be doing this.' So, I ask, 'How come? He didn't say anything to me.' And she says, 'Don't talk. Just follow. That's it. Listen.' My father never touched us. Really, he just looked at you, and that was enough."

From his father, Lionel learned about obligation:

"When you talk about my father, his physical presentation was always straight. He was a small person, but stocky and, always, even to the last few years of his life, he was always pretty straight, maybe bent over somewhat. But, as far as the kind of thinking he had, I can relate to you one of the things that we did as a family. Every year in January, we had a New Year's party at our house. Our company was small — this is National Mortgage — but we had our employees come to our house and my mother and her friends would cook. My brother, my sister and I would serve. This was done because, it was explained to us, to give thanks to those who worked at the company to make

it what it was and to show our appreciation. Now, that's the kind of basic things that happened that affected [me]."

This sense of obligation moved Lionel to get involved in the effort to "Save the Center" — the Japanese Cultural Center of Hawaiʻi — which was facing bankruptcy and the loss of its property and buildings in 2002 and 2003. As Dr. Fujio Matsuda recalls, "Lionel didn't want any publicity for himself. But, if he didn't support us by taking care of the expenses to conduct the fundraising campaign, this whole effort wouldn't have gotten off the ground."

Lionel explained:

"When I was president of the Japanese Chamber, I'd asked Walter Tagawa to come up with a five-year plan. And he came up with this idea. You know, the Chamber does so many things that are not necessarily business-oriented, so he came up with this idea to make another organization, which eventually became JCCH. The whole idea was we had to get property. We raised the money to buy the property and put up the building. So, personally, I was really involved in getting this thing started. And when the financial troubles were revealed and these guys said, 'We going sell it,' I got so mad! I can't believe it. You gotta be joking! That was too embarrassing — to allow something like that to happen. I couldn't believe it!"

With other community leaders, Lionel worked quietly behind the scenes to successfully raise nine million dollars in five months, thereby saving the cultural center and honoring the intentions of the original donors.

From the beginning of this interview, Lionel insisted that he did not know what was "Japanese" and what was otherwise. What is obvious is that he embodies universal values learned throughout his life and that his sense of humor has contributed to his unique character.

After this interview concluded and we got up to leave the room, Lionel put his hands together and bowed to his good friend, Fujio Matsuda. "Always respect your elders," he said. And with that very Japanese gesture, the interview was over.

41

~

Lionel Yukio Tokioka spent his summers learning his family's business from the ground up, delivering messages and cleaning the bank vault after hours. He also worked in the pineapple cannery like most teens his age.

Tokioka was appointed President of International Savings & Loan in 1969. In 1983, he and the company's directors took International Savings & Loan public. In 1999, Tokioka was elected Chairman of CB Bancshares, Inc., which Central Pacific Financial Corporation acquired in 2004.

Although active in business-related organizations, Tokioka has also supported many community organizations, including the Aloha Medical Mission; the Public Schools of Hawaii Foundation; the Hawai'i Community Foundation; the Chamber of Commerce of Hawaii; the Honolulu Japanese Chamber of Commerce, of which he served as President in 1968; and the Japanese Cultural Center of Hawai'i. Tokioka and his wife Carole are the parents of two adult children.

A LIFE OF SERVICE

Shimeji Kanazawa

I come from a big family in Kamuela on the island of Hawai'i. We had eleven children! I was the eldest, born on December 29, 1915. Even with eleven children, my parents, Torazo Ryusaki and Saki Harada Ryusaki, showered us with love and made each of us feel special, like we were their only child. My parents were poor, but they never discussed our family's financial situation in front of us, even when I became an adult.

My mother came to Hawai'i as a "picture bride" from Shizuoka, Japan. She was a very wise woman, and frugal. She worked very hard from early morning until late into the night, making *tōfu*, *aburage*, *konnyaku*, *manjū* and *senbei*. She grew vegetables and raised chickens and pigs, so there was always plenty of food on our kitchen table. With eleven children, though, there was not a single day in twenty years that she did not have to wash diapers.

My father was a self-trained auto mechanic who ran an auto repair garage. There were no hotels or restaurants in Kamuela, so if a car broke down on one of the lonely roads leading to Kona, or North Kohala, or Honoka'a, my father would invite the driver and his passengers to dine with us while he repaired their car. My father was a gregarious man who made friends easily and was always happy to help others. He spoke Hawaiian and English beautifully and conversed with us children in English; our mother spoke Japanese to us and we responded in English, which she came to understand quite well. They both instilled in us a respect for our elders and the importance of extending kindness to friends and strangers alike.

In our family, *ganbare*, the Japanese word for perseverance, was a core value around which we lived our lives. My parents reminded us to always do our best in whatever we undertook and to never expect to be given something for nothing. Keep moving forward, no matter what roadblocks may stand in your way, or regardless of how impossible the situation might appear, they always said.

I attended Waimea Elementary School from 1921 to 1929. There were less than twenty students in our class and we spent the entire day in one classroom with just one teacher. My schoolmates were, for the most part, Hawaiian and Japanese, with a few Chinese. Most of our teachers were Hawaiian or part-Hawaiian.

When it came time for middle school, I was sent far away to Hilo Intermediate School, which I attended from 1929 to 1931. It was a big change from my one-classroom school in tiny Waimea. At Hilo Intermediate, there were three or four homerooms within every grade level and we changed teachers and classrooms every hour or so. For a naïve country girl like me, the change was confusing. As a result, I began to stutter when I spoke.

In my junior year of high school, I was elected student body secretary. My counselor, Mrs. Sarah W. Putnam, who was also the school Vice Principal, was very kind and took me under her wing. She worked with me to develop my self-confidence, and before I knew it, my stuttering had stopped.

My early ambition of becoming either a secretary or a teacher was realized when the Department of Public Instruction (today's Department of Education) hired me as the secretary of Kohala High and Elementary School at the end of summer. However, my tenure with the department was cut short due to the events of December 7, 1941.

In World War II, Sweden was a neutral power. As a result, the Swedish Vice Consul in Hawai'i, Mr. Gustaf W. Olson, was appointed to oversee the Japanese Consulate and Japanese interests in the Islands. But with the large number of civilian casualties and injuries from the December 7 attack, Mr. Olson was overwhelmed in his full-time job as administrator of Queen's Hospital.

"I need a girl to run the Consulate office," he said. "She must speak Japanese, but more important to me is that I find a girl with a 'Red Cross' heart."

Mr. Eldon Morell, Director of the Vocational Division where I worked, recommended me for the Consulate job. Solely on Mr. Morell's recommendation, Mr. Olson hired me, sight unseen, in February of 1942, three months after the attack on Pearl Harbor.

My assignment with the Swedish Vice Consul gave me the rare opportunity to help those in extreme need at a most difficult time. These people inspired me each and every day and brought out the best in me. From them I learned the essence of empathy and developed my caregiving skills. I dedicated myself to doing the best I could for the families that had been torn apart by the war by finding work for the wives whose husbands had been interned; comforting the elderly, who shared their anguish with me; and escorting families to internment camps on the Mainland to be reunited with their husbands and fathers.

Mr. Olson and I also inspected the ships transporting Japanese prisoners of war that stopped in Honolulu en route to the U.S. mainland. We boarded each ship and made certain that the prisoners' living conditions were in compliance with the Geneva Convention, including their food and water, sanitation facilities and recreational activities. We also made sure that they had sufficient medical supplies to last until the ship reached the West Coast. And, we made frequent inspections of the detention camps at Honouliuli and Sand Island to ensure that the detainees were being treated appropriately.

In appreciation for my contributions to the war effort, I was presented a certificate from the national office of the American Red Cross for "Meritorious Performance During World War II." I was also given a trip through thirty-seven states and an all-expenses-paid three-month-long vacation.

Although it was a very generous gesture of appreciation, the greatest gift I received for my war service was the opportunity to help alleviate the suffering of the destitute and the disoriented. That experience helped me to develop an even greater appreciation for the human condition and gave me a chance to treat people in need as my parents had treated each of their eleven children, like we were special.

After returning to Honolulu from my vacation, I met and married my husband, Kinji Kanazawa. Within a month of our marriage, Kinji and I decided to move to Boston so he could enroll in an accelerated two-year law school program at Boston College. I became a student as well, at the Chamberlain School of Retailing, which was a "finishing school" of sorts.

Kinji and I returned to Hawai'i after he received his law degree. He started his practice, specializing in real estate law, and I began working for the Hawai'i Department of Education, providing cooperative retail training to students from McKinley, Kaimukī, Roosevelt and Farrington high schools. Our son, Sidney Kinji, and our daughter, Joni Sakiko, were born soon thereafter.

Once our children were in preschool, I began to engage in volunteer work, in which I found much happiness and purpose in life.

Hawai'i's first chief executive after statehood, Governor William F. Quinn, appointed me to the Commission on Children and Youth. The work of the

Commission led, eventually, to the establishment of the Family Court within the State Judiciary. But it was my next volunteer role that became my life's mission.

In 1963, Governor John A. Burns appointed me to the State of Hawai'i's Commission on Aging. In the years since my appointment, I've witnessed the development of aging programs in Hawai'i. I also took an active role in aging-related activities at the county, state and national level.

The Commission on Aging was responsible for assessing the status and promoting the well-being of older persons. It also served as an advisory body to the Governor and the State Legislature on a range of issues relating to elders.

One of the Commission's priorities in the mid-1970s was the development of a comprehensive master plan for aging in order to address gaps in the various programs and activities for the elderly that were offered by federal, state and local governments, as well as private community groups. An important element in serving the elderly was the creation of the Executive Office on Aging, currently an agency of the State Department of Health, to serve as a catalyst in coordinating programs in Hawai'i.

All across the globe, serious discussions are taking place on subjects such as basic life processes, research on retirement and aging and the explosion of a worldwide population of seasoned adults.

I know of many proposals that sought to enhance the organization of senior programs and the delivery of services. Some were successful, others were not. The issues facing the elderly require timely and substantial attention; thus, I have strongly recommended that the State Executive Office on Aging be a freestanding office. I am glad that the University of Hawai'i has developed a Center on Aging at its Mānoa campus to do research and train future generations of bright and compassionate gerontologists to meet the challenges of Hawai'i's growing population of elders. These efforts will help to foster a more positive self-image among the elderly themselves and improve society's view on aging. In the end, everyone needs to move forward with new skills, new attitudes and a reassessment of values in our changing world.

Additionally, my service on the Board of Trustees of the National Federation of Interfaith Volunteer Caregivers inspired me to start a program in Hawai'i to help the frail elderly and disabled live independently with dignity and for as long as they possibly can. It occurred to me that by developing a caregiving program, our Buddhist community in Hawai'i would be answering the challenge of Monshu Koshin Ohtani, Jodo Shinshu's spiritual leader in Japan, to "break out from the school of isolation, egocentricity and selfishness and become actively concerned with society and its well being." As the Buddhist precept of *Dana* teaches us, we must assist others without desire for acknowledgement or reward. I have tried to follow the course of *Dana* and I credit my many wonderful colleagues for the progress we, together, have made in serving our community.

I am extremely grateful to my family as well, for their unconditional love, support and encouragement allowed me to realize my aspirations and dreams.

As I reflect on my life, I am reminded of how fortunate I have been that doors of opportunity opened to me for education, service and enjoyment. I often think of what a fulfilling journey I have lived — from Kamuela, where I was born, to Mānoa Valley, where I reside. It has been a journey blessed with good fortune, good health, good friends and a remarkable family. *Okagesama de...*

Shimeji Kanazawa, "the girl with 'a Red Cross-heart'" is known simply as "Shim" to her close friends. In 1989, aided by her longtime friend, Rose Nakamura, Kanazawa led the effort to establish Project Dana, an interfaith caregiving program for frail elderly at the Moiliili Hongwanji Mission. The program was founded on the Buddhist precept of *Dana*, or selfless giving.

Kanazawa's contributions to the community have garnered her numerous awards. In 1980, she was recognized by the YWCA of Oʻahu at its annual LeaderLuncheon, and in 1990, the University of Hawaiʻi awarded her an Honorary Doctor of Humane Letters. In 1999, Kanazawa was named a "Living Treasure of Hawaiʻi" by the Honpa Hongwanji Mission of Hawaii, and, in 2012, she was recognized at the Pacific Buddhist Academy's annual "Lighting Our Way" awards banquet as an "Inspirational Leader" for her fidelity to *Dana*. Kanazawa and her late husband Kinji raised two children.

GAKKŌ. GAKUMON. YĀNINJU.

Yoshinobu Oshiro

I was the eighth child in a family with nine children, but I became the youngest when my little brother died at the age of six. Our father was a laborer who was in charge of a crew of irrigators who worked for ʻEwa Sugar Plantation. To supplement the family's income, he raised pigs in an area provided by the plantation until it was demolished for a U.S. Marine Corps airfield. Several months later, a large poultry farm became available near our home, so my parents and older siblings took it over.

My mother managed our home. I was raised in a well-organized home environment in which everyone had a responsibility and met our parents' expectations. My eldest sister, who was fifteen years older than me, became my surrogate mother. She made sure that I did my homework correctly and also helped me communicate with my parents, who spoke no English. My mother and father spoke to each other in Okinawan and Japanese languages, which I did not understand, and also used other ethnic phrases called Pidgin English. While growing up, I remember hearing them speak of the importance of *gakkō* (school), *gakumon* (study, learning) and *yāninju* (Okinawan language for family togetherness). These three words I remember distinctly.

Upon graduating from Waipahu High School in 1946, I answered the call to military service, much to the disappointment of my parents, especially my father — they wanted me to go to college. I tried to appease them by saying that I might be sent to Japan or Okinawa.

I was assigned to the U.S. Army Counterintelligence Corps and, fortunately, was sent to occupied Japan. The Army needed personnel who could communicate in Japanese, so I, along with three hundred other newly enlisted men from Hawai'i, trained at Schofield Barracks on O'ahu for several weeks and then were shipped to Japan. I was among sixty new recruits who were selected to become part of the Allied Translation Interpreter Section (ATIS) in Tōkyō. After taking several accelerated classes in conversational Japanese, including military terminology, we received our individual assignments with various units throughout Japan.

I used the opportunity of a short leave to travel south to Okinawa and after a bit of a search, found both my father's and mother's families. It was a difficult time, as they were still recovering from the devastation of the Battle of Okinawa. I wrote to my parents about my meeting with relatives in Okinawa. They were relieved to receive some news about their relatives.

In all, I spent three years in Japan, questioning former Japanese soldiers and assisting the Home Ministry with the processing of former prisoners of war from Siberia. At the conclusion of my Japan assignment, I returned to Hawai'i.

While being discharged in Hawai'i, I decided to continue my military service by joining the Army Reserve. I would be paid for the time I spent at monthly drills and annual active duty summer camps, which would help me through college.

When I enrolled at the University of Hawai'i (UH) using my GI Bill benefits, I signed up for the newly formed Air Force Reserve Officers' Training Corps (ROTC) on campus. Fortunately, I was allowed to transfer from the Army Reserve to the Air Force Reserve, which provided opportunities for me to be commissioned as an officer.

As the youngest in my family, I was used to receiving unsolicited advice from my older siblings, which I always valued. So when I heard my UH agriculture professor, Dr. Y. Baron Goto, advise a group of students to go to a Mainland school for a broader experience and to increase the chances of being hired for local agricultural jobs, I transferred to the University of Missouri for two years and then returned to UH for my senior year.

While in Missouri, the agribusiness company Libby McNeil and Libby was recruiting agriculture majors to work in Hawai'i. They asked me if I would be willing to move back to Hawai'i to work. "Sure," I said, with a smile on my face.

After graduating from UH with my Bachelor's degree in Agriculture and my commission as a second lieutenant in the Air Force Reserve, I worked for Libby McNeil, assessing pineapple fields for harvesting and supervising the young summer workers on Molokaʻi. My parents were really happy that I was able to find a job in my field of study with a good salary. During my time on Molokaʻi, however, Father fell ill and I returned home to ʻEwa to help my parents with the chicken farm.

The postwar "baby boom" resulted in increased enrollment in Hawaiʻi's public school system, which led to an opportunity I could not refuse. I had a few months of eligibility remaining on my GI Bill, so I used the time to return to school, where I enrolled in a one-year course. They called us "Retreads" because we already had our Bachelor's degree; however, because we could not find work in our majors, they retrained us to become teachers.

I worked on the chicken farm for a year while completing the course. I was then assigned to teach fifth graders at Barbers Point Elementary School. It was not until my next assignment, at ʻEwa Elementary School, that I realized the intrinsic rewards of teaching — where I felt I was giving back to the community that had raised me and where my parents and many family friends still resided.

Around this time, I met and married a fellow teacher, Nancy Tamanaha. Nancy had a Master's degree in teaching. This motivated me to further my credentials as well, so I took a professional improvement leave and enrolled at Los Angeles State College, where I earned my Master's degree.

With that, I returned to the Hawaiʻi Department of Education (DOE) and taught at several schools, eventually moving into the area of educational administration, again on the advice and encouragement of friends and colleagues.

Thanks to Nancy and others, I was able to juggle family, which now included two young children, my school responsibilities and my military reserve duties.

While in the Air Force Reserve, I provided information on teacher hiring, curriculum standards, equal opportunity, credit transfers, cultural adjustments, etc., to the congressional delegation responsible for inspecting military dependents' schools in the Pacific Basin area, mainland Japan and Okinawa, Korea and the Philippines to ensure that the Air Force was fulfilling its duty to provide military dependents with an education equal in quality to what children were receiving in America.

In time, officials with the dependents' schools program encouraged me to pursue my doctorate in education, which I earned in 1974 from Utah State University. The dependents' schools became the focus of my dissertation, which was titled: "Historical Development of the Department of Defense Schools with Emphasis on Japan, Far East-Pacific Area, 1946–1973."

Upon returning from Utah, I became the principal at several different elementary schools on Oʻahu and also spent some time working as an administrator in the State Department of Education.

My World War II service impacted me for life; here is an example. In my first assignment as a teacher at Barbers Point Elementary School, the music teacher and I wanted to build school spirit, so I wrote a song and she added the melody. When I became the principal of Iroquois Point School, the boys basketball team was experiencing an unusually successful season. The girls got caught up in the excitement and wanted to become cheerleaders, but they didn't have any choreographed routines. So I used the music from the Barbers Point School and wrote new lyrics for Iroquois Point School.

So what does this have to do with the Military Intelligence Service? Well, I recycled that melody one more time for a team song for the Military Intelligence Service Club of Hawaii. When the Oahu AJA Veterans Council established the annual Joint Memorial Service, which is held every September, unlike the 100th Infantry Battalion and the 442nd Regimental Combat Team, the MIS did not have a song, so I suggested that something be done about it. The responsibility came right back to me. After some thought, I returned to that old Barbers Point and Iroquois Point spirit song and began writing the lyrics for an MIS song. It was much more work than I thought it would be, as I had to do research on the MIS so that the words would accurately impart the history and legacy of the men and women who had served in the Military Intelligence Service. Needless to say, trying to find words that rhymed with place names like Peleliu, Bataan and Suribachi was somewhat challenging.

Even after Nancy and I retired as principals of DOE schools, we remained involved in education, volunteering and doing consultant work, such as evaluating preschools on Oʻahu and in Tōkyō, Japan. I still feel gratified when former students come up to me and thank me for being their teacher.

In 1992, cancer claimed Nancy's life. Several years later at a Waipahu High School reunion, I met Anna Nabarrete, who, like me, had lost her spouse. We became good friends and, in 2000, we were married. Anna's children and grandchildren live in Washington state and California, so we spend quite a bit of our time visiting them.

I also help my siblings and their families whenever I can. My parents had taught us the Okinawan concept of *yāninju* — helping each other — and that has remained with me all my life. So, whether it's babysitting my granddaughters or helping out my elderly siblings, I do whatever I can.

I also felt a personal obligation to the Air Force Reserve for the many opportunities it provided in my life, so I continued to serve as a Lieutenant Colonel until I retired.

For many years, I held a keen interest in a "host nation" program for overseas military dependent schools. Although the program has undergone changes over the years, I think a valuable part of the military dependents' education is their exposure to the community, language, culture and lifestyle of the community or host nation in which they are presently living.

Another cultural exchange project I have participated in since 1993 is the "International Student Cultural Exchange Program" for middle school students from Haebaru-*cho* (town), my parents' hometown in Okinawa. My family and I and members of our Okinawan locality club help the organizers find local host families for the students and even welcome them into our own homes. It is a wonderful exchange program for both the Okinawa and Hawai'i students. The principal of Washington Middle School welcomed the Haebaru students to his campus to experience a Hawai'i school because he believes it is an excellent way to encourage friendship and understanding and to promote world peace. So, what began as a way of honoring my parents and the hometown they left behind to give us, their children, a good life in America, resulted in the building of many new friendships and enjoyable experiences.

For a school assignment, my granddaughter, Melissa Wong, a Punahou School senior, wrote: "My grandpa believes that it is important to be honest to yourself, as well as to trust your friends. Also, we must not forget that it is a privilege to live in this country…. My grandpa believes that the family is an integral unit. As the youngest, he was loved and cared for very well."

My journey from 'Ewa Plantation can be summed up in this way: Although it was filled with twists and turns, I never felt lost. At significant intersections along the way, my choices were guided by education, my family, trust in my friends and a strong sense of obligation. I appreciate the advice friends shared with me and I will continue to give back to the community, to Haebaru Town and Haebaru Club, to my veteran-comrades and, especially, to my fellow Military Intelligence Service veterans.

~

Yoshinobu Oshiro and his wife Anna have been active in promoting educational student exchanges between Hawai'i and Okinawa, much of which he does as a longtime member of the Haebaru Club Board of Directors. Oshiro is also a member of the Utah State University chapter of Phi Beta Kappa, which is an honor society for education majors.

In 1995, Oshiro served as editor of Yuki Kikuchi's book, "Hawaii Nikkei Nisei no Taiheiyo Senso," ("The Pacific War of the Nisei in Hawaii") which focused on the role Japanese Americans played in the Pacific theater during World War II. In his Editor's Notes, Oshiro said he hoped that the struggle and contributions of Japanese Americans would leave a "legacy of the spirit of '*gambari*' and 'stick-to-itiveness' for the common goal, a legacy that will be remembered for all eternity."

Oshiro has served as an officer and director of the MIS Veterans Club of Hawaii, for whom he wrote the "MIS Team Song." The song recalls many of the fields of battle where Military Intelligence Service veterans served in World War II. In 2011, Oshiro traveled to Washington, D.C., for the presentation of the Congressional Gold Medal to veterans of the 100th Infantry Battalion, 442nd Regimental Combat Team and the Military Intelligence Service.

THE GIFT OF HELPING OTHERS

Lillian E. Yajima

"I expect to pass through this world but once. Any good therefore that I can do, or any kindness or abilities that I can show to any fellow creature, let me do it now. Let me not defer it or neglect it, for I shall not pass this way again."

— *Willam Penn*

Community service has been an important part of Lillian Emiko Nawahine Noda Yajima's life for nearly her entire life.

As a child growing up, doing for others and sharing with the less fortunate was as normal a thing to do as breathing. Lillian's maternal grandmother, Eki Teshima, chose to live independently rather than move in with her daughter Alice — Lillian's mother — and her family after her husband, Yasuke Teshima, passed away. Grandmother Teshima wanted to be independent so that she could continue her volunteer activities, especially caring for the elderly at the home for Japanese men. She explained to Lillian that these men had come to Hawai'i to labor in the sugar plantations and pineapple fields. They had never married and now, in their advanced age, were all alone with no children or other family members to care for them. Grandmother Teshima would take them homemade *kiku* ointment in clamshells, prepare and deliver treats or much-needed personal items and just spend time visiting with the lonely residents there. As a youngster in preschool, Lillian spent a great deal of time with her grandmother, observing the hours of work her grandmother devoted to preparing for her visits to the hospital.

Lillian's mother, Alice Sae Teshima Noda, followed in her mother's footsteps, selflessly devoting much of her time and leadership skills to numerous organizations, including the Girl Scouts, Community Chest (forerunner to the Aloha United Way), the Congress of Parent Teachers Association and the Japanese Women's Society. She also started the beauty culture board of examiners and was one of the first dental hygienists in Honolulu, later supervising the Dental Hygiene School.

Alice Noda also served as the first President of the Japanese Women's Society, where she had an opportunity to work on a project that was near and dear to her heart — the establishment of a care home for elderly women at Kuakini Hospital.

Lillian admired both her mother and her grandmother, for both women taught her through their commitment and actions that helping others made many people happy and was intrinsically rewarding.

Lillian's father, Steere Noda, a Territorial Senator, supported his wife's active involvement in community affairs. He himself became more involved in the community and in sports.

Education was important in the Noda family. Lillian attended Hanahauʻoli School and graduated from Roosevelt English Standard School before matriculating to the University of Hawaiʻi, where she earned her bachelor's degree in sociology and a fifth-year teaching certificate. She continued her education in the ensuing years, enrolling in postgraduate professional development courses in art, music, math, drama, physical education and hula. She also studied Polynesian music and dance at UH.

Lillian's love for hula and her becoming a certified hula instructor has helped her keep fit. She spends much of her time teaching others and performing at nursing homes and at community events. "Performing hula and teaching Hawaiian seed jewelry honors the native host culture of Hawaiʻi and the beauty of our home state," she said. "Besides, since we live in Hawaiʻi, the main thing is to show love and appreciation for our Hawaiian culture."

Prominently displayed in Lillian's bedroom is a quote by William Penn, who founded the British Province of Pennsylvania, which later became the State of Pennsylvania. Lillian's mother clipped the quotation from a newspaper and pasted it on her mirror:

"I expect to pass through this world but once. Any good therefore that I can do, or any kindness or abilities that I can show to any fellow creature, let me do it now. Let me not defer it or neglect it, for I shall not pass this way again."

"I really believe that," said Lillian. "I can't come back, so I have to do it now."

Lillian says she feels good when she has made someone happy, something that was instilled in her as a youngster. As the youngest of four children in the Noda household, her older siblings often gave her simple tasks to do, lavishing praise and appreciation on her as she completed them. Looking back, they were not difficult tasks, but the praise and appreciation motivated her to continue helping her siblings.

Today, Lillian says she is thrilled when she receives thank you letters from people who have benefited from her service — whether it is for teaching them about Japanese culture, or demonstrating *origami* and jack-o'-lantern *manjū*, or organizing a multiethnic cultural program at the Kuakini Care Home. She is grateful to her late husband Tad for supporting her passion and for allowing her to spend so much time caring for others.

Lillian truly believes in the importance of sharing and perpetuating Japanese culture, not only among ethnic Japanese, but with everyone. She hopes that by teaching the rich traditions and values to the younger generation, they will then pass them on to their children. "My wish is that everybody helps a little bit just by doing something Japanese every day," she said.

"Volunteer work is the Girl Scout in me — to help other people wherever I can," she says.

Lillian's daughter, Lenny Andrew, inherited her mother's love for Japanese culture and served for several years as the President and Executive Director of the Japanese Cultural Center of Hawai'i. She continues to volunteer on various projects. And, Lillian's son Tyler supports his wife, Loretta, in her volunteer capacity as President of the Board of Directors of the Children's Discovery Center.

But volunteerism in the Yajima family doesn't end there. Lillian recruited her grandchildren, Kimi and Davey Andrew, to volunteer at the Kuakini Care Home's annual Christmas party, dressing up as Mr. and Mrs. Santa Claus. Davey was five years old and Kimi was three when they first began tagging along with their grandmother, bringing smiles to the faces of the care home residents, some of whom had no family to visit them.

Says Lillian, "It is a family tradition to 'care and volunteer,' which I hope we can carry on for many more generations."

Lillian E. Yajima, who was in her nineties in 2013, continues to teach hula at Hale Pulama Mau at Kuakini Medical Center and at other locations in Honolulu. She also introduced the "Adopt A Mom" program to ensure that the women residents of Hale Pulama Mau are treated to a Mother's Day celebration. Yajima takes the lead in organizing the event, which is sponsored by the Japanese Women's Society Foundation. Yajima remains an active member of and participant in numerous organizations and events, including the Japanese Women's Society Foundation, United Japanese Society of Hawaii, Japanese Cultural Center of Hawai'i and the Cherry Blossom Festival.

In 2007, she was awarded The Order of the Rising Sun, Gold and Silver Rays, from the Government of Japan, and in the spring of 2013, the United Japanese Society presented her with its "UJSH Award for Contributions to the Japanese Community and Hawai'i."

WINDOWS ON LIFE

Wallace T. Fukunaga

I was born in 1937, the youngest of Tadashi and Yoshiko Fukunaga's six children. My father was an *Issei* who had immigrated to Hawai'i as a teen with his older brothers and sister from Iwakuni in Yamaguchi, Japan. My mother, on the other hand, was a *Nisei* who was born and raised in Hawai'i. Like my father, her parents had emigrated from Yamaguchi. Both my parents were Buddhists. They worked hard and instilled in us a strong work ethic and an appreciation for education. My father worked for Meadow Gold Dairies, previously known as Dairymen's, for sixty years. He was a noted *bonsai* enthusiast, a calligrapher and a fisherman, whose regular catches of fresh and delicious fish went a long way in feeding our family.

Hawai'i was a Territory back then and largely rural. I grew up in the Sheridan district of Honolulu and attended McKinley High School, where I was active in student government — I was elected Student Body President in my senior year.

I spent my summers working in the pineapple cannery to help support our family. Many of my classmates worked there as well, so we often laughed with each other while perspiring together. Thanks to the caring of a youth worker at Makiki Christian Church, which was located near my home, several friends and I became Christians while attending a youth camp which we had been invited to by the youth worker.

After graduating from McKinley High School in 1955, I attended Harvard University on a full scholarship. The transition from a public high school to an Ivy League college was a huge challenge for me. But thanks to the support of my family and friends and my Christian faith, I survived and graduated in 1959 with a degree in Far Eastern Studies.

I then enrolled at Princeton Theological Seminary, where I received my Master's degree in Divinity in 1963. While in seminary, I spent a year researching religion in higher education at the University of California at Berkeley on a Danforth Fellowship.

My career path after Seminary took on three distinct stages. Each provided a different window on life and called for a new learning curve. They are as follows:

Stage One: Education and politics (1963–1973). For six years I served as campus minister at the University of Hawai'i at Mānoa and was deeply involved in higher education and the political activism of the 1960s that included the Kalama Valley land struggle, anti-Vietnam War and the civil rights movements of the 1960s. During this period, I also worked at the Hawai'i State Legislature, drafting bills to help the poor and working for a national consulting firm that had been contracted by both the State and Federal governments to reform public housing in Hawai'i. This work in the early stages of my career gave me skills in teaching and planning and an understanding of the importance of justice and peace in our lives.

Stage Two: Entrepreneurship and working on the land (1973–1991). After being in the thick of education and politics, I moved out to Pūpūkea, a community on the north shore of O'ahu, where I lived on an acre and a half of land. There, I started a restaurant business and property management firm called Northshore Resources, Inc. In 1987, WorkHawaii named it "Small Business of the Year." By the time I sold it in 1991, it had fifty-five employees and gross annual sales of $1.8 million. This stage of my life instilled in me the patience and perseverance necessary to start and grow a business. It also offered hands-on lessons in finances and staff development. From the rich Pūpūkea land, I gained practical skills in tilling the earth and having fruits, flowers and vegetables thrive.

Stage Three: Ministry and community service (1991–present). I think of this stage of my life as more centered and integrated. I was also able to put to use the various skills I learned in the previous two stages of my life. I returned to the ministry and served several local congregations as their senior minister, among them The Community Church of Honolulu,

Waiokeola Congregational Church, Moanalua Community Church and Christ Church Uniting in Kailua.

In 1993, I returned to school and earned a Doctor of Ministry degree at the Pacific School of Religion in Berkeley, California. The school presented me its Distinguished Alumnus Award in 2006.

This period of my life heightened my creativity in the realms of spirituality, meditation and writing. Among the new insights I gained is that Christianity has no monopoly on Jesus. Buddhists understood him as a *bodhisattva*, Hindus as an avatar, and both Muslims and Jews as a prophet from God. I have also gained a deeper appreciation for the performing arts, world cultures and religions and international travel. Meditation, exercise, *qigong* massage therapy and holistic healing have all become integral activities in my daily life. They have all led to an abiding sense of inner peace.

This phase has also been marked with broader community service. I served on the Board of Trustees of the Pacific School of Religion in Berkeley; on the Board of Governors of the Japanese Cultural Center of Hawaiʻi; and on the boards of the Hawaiʻi Conference of the United Church of Christ, the Honolulu chapter of the Japanese American Citizens League, American Civil Liberties Union and the Mental Health Association of Hawaii. For a time I served as the interim executive director of the Counseling & Spiritual Care Center of Hawaiʻi and I now serve on the board of the Interfaith Alliance of Honolulu, chairing its Commission on Community Building. I am also a member of the State of Hawaiʻi Civil Rights Commission.

I attribute the shaping of my character and the accomplishments in my life to four major influences: my parents and Japanese upbringing, my education, religion and Hawaiʻi's multiculturalism. My parents and my Japanese upbringing instilled in me values that uphold the importance of family, work and community. The education I received taught me to think critically and creatively and offered opportunities for meaningful work. My religion opened my consciousness to a presence greater than myself that embraces a universal and transcendent mercy and hope. And, Hawaiʻi's multiculturalism taught me the importance of *aloha*, which honors the sacred in all people and life and celebrates diversity.

My life has been richly blessed and I am now eager to share my blessings with others and the world. I regard the invitation to share this biographical sketch as an important way of doing that.

~

Wallace T. Fukunaga has lived a full life as a religious scholar, a social and civil rights activist, an entrepreneur, a farmer, a practicing minister and a nonprofit executive.

Fukunaga founded the Sunrise Ministry Foundation and has been a pastor at numerous United Church of Christ churches, including one in Waimea, Kaua'i. He was Interim Executive Director of the Counseling & Spiritual Care Center of Hawai'i until Spring 2013.

In 2006, the Pacific School of Religion in Berkeley, California, presented a "Distinguished Alumni Award" to Fukunaga, noting that he "connects his faith to matters of justice, tolerance and peace."

Fukunaga is a former President of the American Civil Liberties Union, Hawai'i Chapter, and is currently a member of the Hawai'i Civil Rights Commission. Additionally, he has served on the boards of the Japanese American Citizens League-Honolulu Chapter, Mental Health Association of Hawaii, Waikiki Health Center, the Interfaith Alliance Hawaii and the Japanese Cultural Center of Hawai'i Board of Governors.

ALWAYS SAY "I CAN"

Seichi Tabata

I started a *judō dōjō*, a practice hall, in Lahaina, Maui, after the captain of the Lahaina police station asked me to help him with some of the troubled youth in the area. Lahaina was a high-crime district at the time — there were many stabbings and burglaries and other crimes.

My father, Shozo Tabata, got me started in *judō* when I was nine years old. He thought it would be an effective way to restore my health. When I was three, I contracted measles and became very ill. I later developed an asthma condition. From then on, I was a very sickly child.

When I turned nine years old, my father began sending me to *judō* classes. The training was a big help. Practicing *judō* helped to restore my health and improve my self-confidence. *Judō* became a way of life for me and helped me to develop my strength.

Knowing that *judō* had made such a major difference in my life, I knew that its discipline could help the kids improve their lives, so I told the Lahaina police captain to send the kids over to my *dōjō*. About a hundred boys turned up for my *judō* class — they certainly were a band of rascals! But as I worked with them and trained them, I noticed that their behavior began to improve. In fact, when I took the kids to Hilo for a *judō* tournament at the Hilo Hongwanji, where we stayed, our hosts were pleasantly surprised by the kids' behavior. The boys didn't have a good reputation going in, so our hosts wondered whether the kids would damage their *dōjō*. Much to their surprise, however, the kids took good care of the *dōjō*, cleaned it and left it just as they had found it.

These once-troubled youngsters also began to experience success in their own personal lives. *Judō* had taught them discipline and instilled in them a positive outlook. It had helped them build self-confidence.

The year 1953 changed my life forever. In that year, I met Koichi Tohei-Sensei for the first time. He would become my greatest mentor. My father told me that he had read about a small, but very strong and powerful man from Japan. He was only five-foot-three-inches tall and weighed one-hundred-forty-five pounds, but he could throw a person with his fingers. I was interested in seeing this man in action, so my top *judō* student, Solomon Naleieha, and I went to see Tohei-Sensei's exhibition. *Sensei* noticed me and asked me to participate in his exhibition. He had incredible rhythm and easily threw me. I was very impressed.

I invited Tohei-Sensei to come to Lahaina to share his teachings with my *judō* students. I was interested in learning more from him, as well.

Not everyone was as impressed with *Sensei* as I was, however. The head of the martial arts schools on Maui told Tohei-Sensei not to come because no one was interested in what he had to teach.

Tohei-Sensei remembered that I had invited him to come to Lahaina to teach *aikidō* and *ki* to my *judō* students. We trained with him for a month and then he returned to Japan. Even my father, who had kidney problems at the time, trained with *Sensei*.

What is *ki*, you are probably wondering. *Ki* is the power of the universe. Human beings only see what their eyes can see. For example, when we see a man who is six-feet-five-inches tall and two-hundred-eighty pounds, we immediately think that he is a strong man. Most likely he is physically strong. But a man can be small and still possess internal strength. He can be strong like an iceberg. An iceberg appears small above the surface of the ocean. Below the ocean's surface, however, the iceberg is a huge mass of ice as much as a hundred times larger than what can be seen above the water. That's why the nine-hundred-ton luxury liner *Titanic* sank in 1912. It was thought that because the iceberg was rather small, the ship could safely continue on its voyage to New York. But the ice below the surface of the water was huge and it damaged the ship so severely that it sank within three hours of scraping the iceberg.

Tohei-Sensei returned to Lahaina several times in the ensuing years to teach us more *aikidō* and *ki*. Four years after *Sensei* started coming to Lahaina, I began teaching *aikidō* five days a week and *judō* twice a week. In 1960, I achieved *Sandan*, or third rank, in *judō*.

My wife Emiko began studying *aikidō* with me and became my best assistant instructor in the art. In 1975, she began traveling with me to Japan so we could both train with Tohei-Sensei. She earned the rank of *Rokudan*, or sixth rank, in *Shin Shin Toitsu Aikidō* and became an assistant lecturer for the Ki Society. Emiko also traveled with me to Oregon and Canada, where we helped our son Calvin train his students in *aikidō* and *ki*.

Tohei-Sensei's teachings were truly impressive. He was the first person to teach *aikidō* and *ki* outside of Japan. In the 1960s, *Sensei* traveled to the mainland United States to open practice halls, and later to Europe and other locations around the world. He founded the International Ki Society and spread the teaching of *ki* around the world.

We are fortunate that Tohei-Sensei came to Hawai'i to teach *aikidō*. He died in 2011. Someone like him comes into our universe and our lives once in five-hundred years. He inspired me to accomplish many things. I'm grateful for all that he shared with me.

Tohei-Sensei taught me that human beings have great power and potential, and that is what I try to pass on to my students. We must put our power and potential to good use.

Ki is a life art. We need to study it and make it a part of everything we do in our lives. *Ki* teaches us to always think and act positively. Never say, "I cannot" — always say, "I can." Challenge yourself. You lose before you even start if you say "I cannot." If you say, "I can," you embrace the possibility to succeed in whatever you undertake.

Seichi Tabata, who is the last of Koichi Tohei-Sensei's original students, is the chief instructor and an Eighth *Dan* in *Shin Shin Toitsu Aikidō*. Tabata, who was well into his eighties in 2013, continued to practice, study and teach *aikidō* and *ki* at the Honolulu Ki Society's Seishinkan *Dōjō* in Nu'uanu. In 2013, Tabata marked sixty years of teaching *Shin Shin Toitsu Aikidō* in Hawai'i.

Tabata authored a book on *ki*, *Shin Shin Toitsu Aikidō* and *kiatsu*. Seichi and Emiko Tabata raised four children. Emiko Tabata, her husband's trusted assistant and a Sixth *Dan* black belt instructor for the Honolulu Ki Society, passed away in 2009.

LIVING ʻOHANA

Jane F. Serikaku

My parents always stressed the importance of education, no matter how difficult the times were for us with nine children in our family. In this day and age, we would be considered a family in financial need and would have qualified for free lunch and food stamps if those programs had been available back then — that's how destitute we were. But we never knew it because we lived on a farm: You grow your own veggies and you go down to the ocean to get fish. We thought we were fine.

Because public school education was free up through high school, my parents were very straightforward with us: They told us that they could not afford to send us to college, so we knew we would have to find some way to do it. But they always instilled in us that education was important, especially for a woman. "Be a teacher or a nurse," they said, because that's all there was for women back then; nothing else was acceptable.

At the time, we were living on a two-acre farm in Māliko Gulch, on the eastern side of the island of Maui. I was a member of the 4-H Club and raised a beef steer — you get it as a young calf and you raise that steer. Then we would auction it off at the Maui County Fair and get a thousand dollars for the steer. Everything I earned through my 4-H Club projects was banked for my college education. That's how I was able to go to the University of Hawaiʻi. I did that for a number of years. If I wanted to go to college, I had to find some way to do it, and that was my way.

I credit my parents for instilling in us the desire and capacity to *gaman* — to endure hardship — and to *ganbaru* — to persevere — because no matter what people say, as long as you believe in yourself and you work hard, you can achieve whatever you want. That has stayed with me all my life.

So many opportunities became available to me because of my 4-H Club. It was while in the club that I began to acquire leadership skills and to expand my capacity to work with others and encourage younger people. It used to make me feel good.

I became a junior leader when I was in high school — we would help elementary school students. It just felt good that they could learn and that we could help them to become, not necessarily better students, but better citizens. I think that was when I began thinking about becoming an educator. In elementary school, I had read nothing but nursing books, like the Sue Barton series, so I was into nursing at first. When I started working with younger children, that's when I made the decision to go into education.

I became a teacher and, eventually, the principal of ʻIliahi Elementary School in Wahiawā.

I spent sixteen years at ʻIliahi — they were the most wonderful sixteen years of my life. It was such a challenge, but we really worked hard in trying to make ʻIliahi a community school — for the community, and getting all the people and parents involved. I think it worked — it worked really well — because it became a real ʻohana. The teachers really did all they could to help the kids. We tried to be creative and innovative, because we had a lot of children who were financially disadvantaged, who came from families where they were staying with Grandma because both parents were incarcerated. There were other situations in which the kids had to deal with so much. Then, of course, the teachers had to deal with that. But we tried to develop this ʻohana effort of helping each other.

I think in that sense, we were successful in providing many opportunities for the students, not only in academics, but we also had an ʻukulele group, and hula, too. We did all kinds of things so that the students could develop in a total fashion. I think it helped because the students then became more self-assured. You could tell from the test scores. We started getting better and better. People wanted to come; they wanted to send their kids to our school because of the opportunities we provided and because we had caring teachers. I was blessed. We had the best teachers; even the special-needs teachers — they were all outstanding. It's just working together.

I really believe that no matter what you do, you need to have this ʻohana, this sense of being a family to get where you want to go. I think that's what was successful at 'Iliahi. And, only because of the students, the parents, the teachers — only because of their willingness to work with me — did I receive the Milken Award. That award is really for everybody at 'Iliahi.

I retired from the State Department of Education in 2004. Retirement has given me the opportunity to get much more involved in an organization I am passionate about, the Hawaii United Okinawa Association. I was involved with the HUOA when I was with the DOE, although to a lesser degree because my time was limited due to my school responsibilities. In spite of that, I was honored to serve as president of the HUOA in 1992. I was the organization's first woman president!

That was quite a challenge for myself as well as the government officials in Okinawa, who had never worked with a female president before. So it was a challenge, but one that we both overcame and benefited from.

I think my love for my Okinawan heritage goes back to my childhood. Growing up on Maui during World War II, I distinctly remember my parents hiding or destroying their precious Okinawan and Japanese belongings. All of the Japanese-language schools closed, so I never got a chance to learn Japanese. I think our culture was kind of suppressed. We were all trying to be Americanized. It was only after the war, when I was in the fifth grade, that my mom gave me the opportunity to learn Okinawan dance.

There was a Marine camp near our farm — the troops used to conduct their maneuvers in our banana fields — which was probably why my parents felt compelled to show their allegiance to the United States. My mother stopped singing "*Kimigayo*," the national anthem of Japan, which I often heard her singing as she did her chores. It must have torn her, really, because that song was part of her.

I think it was much more difficult for my parents because they saw themselves, actually, as Japanese, and yet, they couldn't be Japanese — they had to be American. So, there was a change in our home, where they kind of encouraged us to be more American. They wanted us to accept that part of us, I guess. They used to talk a lot about Japan and Okinawa — more Okinawa, of course — and then, all of a sudden, they stopped.

Okinawa was very dear to my parents, who were *Issei* (first-generation immigrant). After all, it was their homeland — they were born there and had grown up there. I remember that when I was in elementary school, a call went out to all of the Okinawan families, asking them to help Okinawa because it had been decimated during the war. That whole area where my parents and their families were from in Okinawa had been bombarded.

On Maui, all of the Okinawan families were very close. If there was any need, all of the families got together to help. So, everyone was sending food and clothing, and us kids, we didn't understand, because everything is going to Okinawa and we have to make do with the very little that was left. But now I understand what my parents and the other families were doing, and I truly appreciate what my parents did for the families in Okinawa.

A short time after retiring from the DOE, I was offered my current position as Executive Director of the Hawaii United Okinawa Association. I don't really think of it as a "job," because I really love what I do. This is very different from a "job," because my work involves my cultural heritage, which I treasure and am very proud of.

I also view it as an opportunity to involve younger people, to help open their eyes to their culture — or if they are not Okinawan, to share the beauty of Okinawan culture with them.

Because of my belief in young people and in the importance of getting them involved, I started a young leaders study tour to Okinawa in which the cost of the participant's travel is shared by the HUOA, the participant, and his or her locality club. I took the first group to Okinawa in 1993. The whole point of it was to immerse them in the Okinawan way of life, so, besides going on tours, they homestay with their relatives there for a few days. When they come back, they at least have a sense of being *Uchinanchu* (person of Okinawan ancestry in Okinawan language).

It worked! Since that first leadership tour, there have been numerous leadership groups and we see our HUOA leaders coming up from those groups. They have a sense of "giving back" — to their own locality club and to HUOA, because it supported their trip. Many of them choose to continue being involved because they feel that sense of being *Uchinanchu* and want to help promote it. So, I think that's one of the really good things that has happened in trying to get younger people involved. That is still my goal — to get younger people involved.

Postscript: In 1998, Jane Serikaku was presented the Milken Educator Award by the Milken Family Foundation. The award, which Teacher Magazine *hailed as the "Oscars of Teaching," was established in 1985 to celebrate, elevate and activate excellence in the teaching profession.*

Lowell Milken, founder of the Milken Educator Award, explained the essence of the award on the Foundation's website: "Each of us can recall those teachers who had a profound impact on our lives, infusing us with their passion for the subjects they taught, providing us with the security to learn from both successes and failures, and challenging us to perform at the peak of our abilities.

"All too often our society allows these educators to go through life unheralded and underappreciated for the critical roles they play in strengthening not just our neighborhoods, but our nation. In truth, such exceptional individuals deserve to be praised, celebrated and rewarded for their enduring role in realizing human potential."

Of Jane Serikaku's selection for the award, the Milken Family Foundation stated: "When Jane Serikaku, principal of Iliahi Elementary School in Wahiawa, began considering a year-round modified schedule, she solicited input not only from her staff but from students and parents as well. This collaborative approach informs much of Ms. Serikaku's work at Iliahi, a linguistically diverse school, fifty percent of whose students qualify for Title I programs. She has successfully implemented Hawaii's Success Compact reading program and has involved the community through projects such as Showcase of Stars and the Invention Convention, which provides students the opportunity to present their work to the community. In 1992, Ms. Serikaku established a free preschool at Iliahi called "Ka Nani O Keiki (The Beauty of the Child)."

Jane F. Serikaku oversees the day-to-day operations of the Hawaii United Okinawa Association (HUOA) and its home, the Hawaii Okinawa Center. The HUOA represents some 40,000 individual members statewide who are organized into forty-nine member-clubs, most of them based on the home towns and villages of their ancestors in Okinawa. Serikaku also coordinates the Okinawa-Hawai'i High School Student Exchange, a partnership between the Hawai'i and Okinawa departments of education. The program gives high school students in Hawai'i and Okinawa an opportunity to learn about each other's homeland and culture through an exchange and homestay program.

Serikaku's only child, Michelle Akemi Whaley, Ph.D., a professor of cell biology and genetics at the University of Notre Dame, is her mother's pride and joy. Says Serikaku: "She is a true example of her grandparents' belief in *gambare*."

THINGS MY MOTHER TAUGHT ME

Fujio Matsuda

I, along with a number of other Hawaiʻi-born Americans of Japanese ancestry (AJAs), was asked by Bishop Ryokan Ara, the prime mover of this project, to contribute my life experiences and thoughts to this book. "Who helped you along the way? What were the cultural values that profoundly impacted you?" Bishop Ara wanted to know.

This is my story. It is told in two parts: a) My cultural metamorphosis, from an immigrant son to an American citizen and how it was shaped by people and events, a cultural autobiography, if you will; and b) An example of a decision I had to make that was shaped by my values.

The Beginning

My father, the third son in his family, immigrated to Hawaiʻi in 1919 to join his father, who worked for the Robinson Sugar Plantation on Kauaʻi. He was 19 at the time, a middle school graduate and a free soul. He soon got into trouble with the plantation management for participating in labor unrest among disgruntled immigrant workers, mostly Japanese and Filipino, was fired and forced to relocate to urban Honolulu.

He worked for a time as a reporter for the *Nippu Jiji*, a local Japanese-language newspaper, where he met and married my mother. She was the fifth daughter in a family of nine children and had only a sixth-grade education. But between she and my father, she turned out to be the one with the business acumen. They opened a restaurant in Kakaʻako's Magoon Block. The restaurant was successful for a time, but failed during the Great Depression. My father learned to repair automobiles as a body and fender man. He fixed damaged sheet metal on cars at Liberty Auto Shop. Being ambidextrous, he could work with both hands to smooth out the crumpled sheet metal and became very skilled in this craft.

My mother worked at the neighborhood tuna packing factory and did part-time work as a maid. They eventually opened a Chinese noodle restaurant, which became very successful. A recipe learned from a Chinese cook who worked in the failed restaurant and modified by my mother by adding Japanese soup stock ingredients proved a huge success. The *saimin* noodles and *wonton* (meat-filled dumplings) were Chinese, and the *udon* noodles were Japanese. Meat sticks marinated in Japanese soy sauce and broiled over charcoal fire completed the menu. The customers were mainly native Hawaiians and Portuguese and Japanese immigrants.

It was a family business, so everyone helped. My three sisters helped out while going to school and, later, while working full-time at their day jobs. They helped to prepare the ingredients and to cook and serve the noodles after school or work. My mother was the "general manager." She did the procurement of all the supplies, paid bills and tended to the customers when my sisters were not available. My father preferred to work in the background, making the noodles and *wonton* during the day, broiling the meat sticks and washing the dishes. When I was old enough, I helped with the *saimin*-making part, always in the morning, and only when school was out. Everyone understood that study was my top priority.

My sisters Janet, Betty and Nancy led full lives with little time for teenage so-cialization. I led the privileged life of an only son, but my sisters never resented it and, in fact, helped my mother spoil me. In their lifetimes, I never heard a single complaint about poverty and hardship from my parents or sisters, only words of hope and encouragement that hard work will change things for the better.

And it did, not that we became rich. Nancy married after finishing business college; Janet and Betty never married. At the end of their lives, our parents lived in a modest home in middle-class Kaimukī that Janet and Betty helped to buy. They were always supportive and caring of me, long after their "kid brother" had grown up and, after Mother died, took over mothering me. In later years, I tried to look after their needs. I am forever grateful for the wonderful, close family life we shared. Our children and grandchildren were an integral part of that intimacy. When the aunties passed away, all of their personal belongings and assets were divided equally among Nancy's kids and my kids, the children they never had.

Growing Up in Kaka'ako

My early life was Japanese in culture and language; my parents did not speak English. We lived in a predominantly Japanese immigrant community. My mother taught me the essence of Japanese culture by the way she lived her daily life: *Nasake*, or compassion, was important to her. *Shōjiki*, honesty; *doryoku*, diligence; *benkyō*, study; *omoiyari*, consideration of others; *gaman*, forbearance or perseverance; *kansha*, gratitude; *okagesama de*, thanks to you; *on*, a debt of gratitude; *giri*, obligation; *haji*, shame; *sonkei*, respect, especially of elders and teachers — these words were used in everyday conversation, repeatedly. These are the values I learned at home. Culturally speaking, the Matsudas were Meiji-era Japanese living in a multicultural environment not found in their native Japan.

Hawaiianization

My world expanded when I entered Pohukaina, a neighborhood public elementary school. The children of other immigrants — Portuguese, Chinese, Filipino, a few Caucasians — and, of course, native Hawaiians, were my classmates. Pidgin English, a mixture of mostly English and Hawaiian words, with some Chinese, Portuguese and Japanese thrown in, served as our medium of communication. We loved Pidgin, while "proper English" was an affectation for classroom use. English was a foreign language that we acquired painstakingly, word by word, following strict rules.

We learned Hawaiian songs and lore. I still remember some of the Hawaiian songs I learned from Mrs. Sea, who was our homeroom teacher and the school's Hawaiian music specialist. The songs were old, of course, and are hardly heard anymore — "*Imi Au Ia 'Oe*" and "*Mai Poina 'Oe Ia'au*." Beautiful songs of old Hawai'i. I have only a garbled memory of the words — I never knew what they meant. The beautiful melodies I do remember, though.

A few years ago, I attended a memorial service for Gladys Brandt, a good Hawaiian friend, at Kawaiaha'o Church. She was a prominent member of the Hawaiian community. The church was full of leaders from the Hawaiian community. All of the songs sung that day were in Hawaiian. Some were familiar to me. But when the congregation sang "*Mai Poina 'Oe Ia'au*," it sounded so beautiful, in a way that only Hawaiians can sing that song. I surprised myself when I found myself singing along; most of the words came back to me from my days in Mrs. Sea's class.

My cultural transition was not from Japanese directly to American, but first to modern Hawaiian, a unique mix of Polynesian, Western and Eastern cultures in a plutocratic agricultural/industrial maritime society in the middle of the Pacific Ocean. The economic and social elites were largely Hawaiian royalty and descendants of New England missionaries and other Caucasian businessmen. I do not remember any racial tension or trouble while growing up in Kakaʻako, although it had a reputation for being a tough district. It was a perception held by outsiders, for we felt secure in our enclave, surrounded by people we knew.

I cannot emphasize enough the importance of Hawaiian culture in the Americanization of the Japanese immigrants and their descendants who settled in Hawaiʻi. The two cultures share many values in common. We both have strong family traditions and value old traditions. Both feel close ties to nature and natural beings, plants and animals. We are both natural environmentalists and conservationists.

Americanization

My Americanization must have begun in elementary school, but what I remember began at McKinley High School. Mrs. Keys, my speech teacher, in her large hat and infinitely patient and sweet way, tried to wean us from Pidgin English so we could be understood by other Americans. Mrs. Wilfong, my junior-year English teacher, taught us how to diagram and analyze sentences, an important tool in understanding the English sentence structure. Mrs. Griegs, my senior homeroom teacher, taught social studies. From her, we learned American history and about democracy, government, citizenship and what it means to be an American. We practiced good citizenship on campus; we voted and participated in student government. They, and other teachers, were preparing us to become productive citizens of our community. It was also in high school that I discovered the logical beauty of mathematics from Mr. Hluboky and Mrs. Logan-Smith, and the fascination of science from Mr. Dorsey.

McKinley was basically a school for the children of immigrants, mostly AJAs, and thus was called "Tokyo High" by people to whom all Asians looked alike.

Pearl Harbor and World War II

Pearl Harbor not only destroyed the U.S. Pacific Fleet on December 7, 1941: It burst open the feudal cocoon within which we lived — poor, but safe, destined to serve the needs of the "Big Five" oligarchy, although I was blissfully unaware of the nature of Hawaiian society. I was a senior at McKinley, Class of 1942. I joined the 442nd Regimental Combat Team (RCT) in March 1943, one of 2,000 volunteers from Hawai'i, all AJAs. Much has been written about this period, so I will not dwell on this historic event.

About nine months into basic training at Camp Shelby, Mississippi, I was transferred to the Army Specialized Training Program (ASTP) in Auburn, Alabama, then to the 291st Field Artillery Observation Battalion for basic training in Camp Gordon, Georgia. The Army worked in mysterious ways, and my life was changed completely. My Americanization shifted into high gear. I was the only *Nisei*, and Asian, among Mainland white soldiers. The 291st was sent to Northern Europe after basic training, where we served until the war ended.

I returned home in December 1945. I will skip the details of my Army service, except to say that serving in the Army with comrades from virtually every state in the union was a unique liberal education in American culture for me. Inevitably, I am asked, was I subjected to racial discrimination in the Army? My answer is, "Not to my knowledge." Perhaps I was too innocent, trusting or simply obtuse to understand the insult. Curiosity, yes, for I was an oddity. Most of them had never known a Japanese American. On the other hand, my comrades who came from all over white America were an oddity to me, as well.

The only white Americans I knew in Hawai'i were my teachers; I had no *haole* friends. In the segregated Army of World War II, we had no blacks. I guess I was technically "not black," which put me in a white Army unit. My Hawaiian multicultural upbringing put me at ease among my new multicultural comrades. We became good friends: Frank Hoar from Boston; Chuck Bade from Detroit; Cal Crandall from Moscow, Idaho; Jim Ryan from San Antonio, Texas; Paul DeLong from Oklahoma; Bob Stoelker from Philadelphia; and a bunch of southerners — Carroll McCollough, John Daugherty, John Newlin, Orlando Covert, Denam Nally, Harold Franks and many more. We were all in the same platoon.

I was made a squad leader, which says a lot about discrimination, or lack thereof, in the Army. Lieutenant Bailey Merrill was our platoon commander. He was a lawyer by profession and a teacher by inclination. We became not just comrades-in-arms, but close friends. By the time the war in Europe ended, some of us had spent about two years together. I learned from my Army friends that people are fundamentally alike; they come in all types and sizes, speak different dialects, have different likes and dislikes, but we all share the basic human traits that foster coexistence and cooperation. We laughed at the same jokes and sang the same traditional songs. I learned many four-letter words that became part of my Army vocabulary, to be avoided in mixed company. Most of my comrades are gone now, including Bailey and Frank, two of my closest friends during and after the war. I just received a Christmas card from Cal Crandall, who retired to California. We have kept in touch for over sixty years.

College

I resumed my life as a student at the University of Hawai'i in familiar, comfortable surroundings. At the end of my sophomore year, I decided to transfer to a Mainland college, something unthinkable before the war, but with the GI Bill to finance my college education and my broadened cultural outlook, it was an easy transition.

Bailey Merrill helped me find a good engineering college, Rose Polytechnic Institute in Terre Haute, Indiana, close to where he lived and practiced law in Evansville. My classmates and colleagues were a different slice of white America from my buddies in the Army, but it reaffirmed my view of human beings in general — we are all different, but we share fundamental values.

Professor Ed McLean was the head of the Department of Civil Engineering; he became my favorite professor and mentor. *Okagesama de*, because of his urging, I decided to continue on to graduate school. With his advice I applied to Yale and MIT (Massachusetts Institute of Technology). I chose MIT, although I was accepted at both schools, attesting to the quality of education at Rose Poly, which was an excellent undergraduate engineering college. For the past several years in a row, *U.S. News and World Report* has ranked it the top small (no doctoral program) engineering college in America.

In June 1949, I returned to Hawai'i to marry Amy Saiki, a McKinley Class of '43 graduate. That was sixty-three years (in 2013) and six children ago. I called Bailey to let him know that I would be stopping in Evansville to introduce my new bride to him and his wife Josephine on our way to MIT. He said, "Great! We'll drive you there." I was sure he misunderstood and started to explain, to which he said, "I know where MIT is; Jo and I will drive you there." We always joked about our chaperoned honeymoon to Niagara Falls, Canada (Toronto, Montreal and Quebec) and down the Maine coast to Boston. He was like the older brother I never had.

Bailey later became an Eisenhower Republican in the U.S. Congress. He once escorted my father and me through the House chambers and onto the floor, where only members are allowed when the House of Representatives is in session. What a thrill it was for an immigrant and his second-generation son. We exchanged visits many times since, Honolulu and Evansville. When our grandson Nathan married Jen in Nashville two years ago, two of our children accompanied us. We took that occasion to visit Bailey's and Jo's grave in Evansville. They had known "Uncle Bailey" and "Aunty Jo," who had never had their own children, but did have six *hānai* Matsuda children.

I ended up spending five years at MIT — three years as a graduate student, two-and-a-half of those as a half-time research assistant, then two more years as a full-time research engineer after earning my doctorate. I thoroughly enjoyed research and decided to make it my career in combination with teaching. Three of our six children were born in Boston, so we have strong ties to New England.

I have had the great good fortune throughout my life of meeting and being helped by wonderful mentors and colleagues who became lifelong friends. Some of them from my high school and Army years I have already mentioned. In addition, there was Dr. Ken Watanabe, my math professor at UH. He was a brilliant Caltech (California Institute of Technology) theoretical physicist, who encouraged me in my studies of math and physics. Bailey Merrill and Ed McLean, I have already mentioned. Don Shimazu, Al Yee, Tets Mitsuda, Ben Ranada and Shinji Soneda, classmates from Rose Poly, became lifelong friends and professional colleagues. Dr. Chuck Norris, my professor of structural engineering at MIT and advisor and mentor at MIT, guided me through graduate school and introduced me to the exciting field of research.

In addition to Chuck Norris, I am deeply indebted to Professors Chris Holley (Structures), Arthur von Ippen (Hydraulics), T. W. Lambe, (Soil Mechanics) and F. B. Hildebrand (Advanced Mathematics), who, together with many others, opened my eyes and mind to the breadth and depth of engineering science. Bob Hansen led the experimental research team on structural dynamics at MIT. I met many kindred souls from all over the U.S. and many foreign countries: Bob Whitman, Bill Wells, Joe Penzien, John Archer, Jack Cord and Y.C. Loh from China; Gerry Galletley from England; Andy Ofjord from Norway; and others were colleagues who enriched my MIT experience. In addition to on-campus laboratory experiments, field research took members of our team to the high deserts of Nevada and the Pacific atolls, a once in a lifetime experience for all on the team.

After completing my research project, I was able to continue my work under Nate Newmark, legendary in our field and head of the Talbot Laboratory at the University of Illinois. We became good friends, though he, too, is gone now. I marveled at his ability to cut to the quick and his ability to identify the critical issues and suggest the options available. He was a founding member of the National Academy of Engineering and one of only a handful of individuals who belonged to both the National Academy of Sciences and the National Academy of Engineering.

I thought my work there would last for some time, but I returned to Hawai'i a year later, rather unexpectedly. I had always wanted to get back to Hawai'i and I just could not forego the chance to do so when the offer came. I continued on the project on a consulting basis for another two years under Nate's guidance until the project's completion.

In 1955, Jasper Holmes, a retired Navy captain and Dean of the College of Engineering, hired me to come back to the University of Hawai'i. For that alone, I owe him a deep debt of gratitude. He was my boss and mentor, and I learned a bit about the University administration at the department level when I was appointed Chairman of the Civil Engineering Department in 1959.

Government Service

In 1962, John A. Burns, newly elected Governor of Hawai'i, asked me to join his cabinet as the Director of the State Department of Transportation (DOT) with responsibility for the airports, harbors, and highways facilities and operations statewide. DOT was one of the largest departments in State government. After consulting with Amy, and Dean Holmes, I accepted the invitation and received a two-year leave of absence from the UH. My thought was that I would put my academic career on hold for two years to perform this public service, a solemn obligation that my parents taught us that we owe to Hawai'i. It meant a substantial loss in income because I had to terminate a partnership in an engineering firm that Don Shimazu and I had formed a few years earlier. A complete severance was required in order to avoid any possible conflict of interest going forward.

We had five children by then, with the sixth on the way, but my wife urged me to do my civic duty; she said she would manage the home front. I must admit that I felt a bit noble for making a family sacrifice to meet that obligation. To be fair, the primary burden of juggling the budget fell on Amy, but it gave me a warm feeling anyway.

Little did I realize then that the Governor was offering me a huge opportunity, not only to contribute to Hawai'i, but also to broaden my horizon and learn about our society, its people and its problems. He was offering me a post-doc in democracy. Jack Burns, whom I did not know personally before our meeting, was a visionary who understood people and their desires and aspirations. He also knew the dark side of life, having served on the police vice squad. I, by comparison, was a wet-behind-the-ears novice in the arena of public affairs, having spent all of my postwar years in academia, involved in ideas and theory, not practicalities and people. He had a strong belief and faith in the people of Hawai'i and their potential to meet the challenges of building a democratic society in Hawai'i. Jack Burns taught me about the nobility of public service, how to be steadfast in your own values and beliefs, and how to absorb disappointments and defeat without giving up, all in the interest of the public you serve. He was the greatest mentor in my life and I did not realize it until years later.

Government service was a new experience. Contrary to common belief, most of the people I met and worked with were competent, dedicated individuals, working in a suffocating bureaucratic environment. The legislators seemed to be a different breed, but I found that they, too, were mostly good people. Having to run for re-election every two or four years changes their behavior pattern, as it would anyone who has to reapply for his or her job every two or four years, open to anyone who wants it and elected by an often uninformed public. I am grateful that I had the good fortune of working with so many dedicated public employees throughout government, including legislators. Of course, there were exceptions among them, as there are in any group of people.

The State was entering a period of unprecedented growth. DOT faced state-wide expansion of its airports, harbors and highways, quite beyond my experience in scope, volume and dollars. I had a tiger by the tail and could not let go. Two years passed in the wink of an eye; I asked for and received a one-year extension of my leave. I was only avoiding the obvious; I resigned before the year was up, giving up my hope of returning to the University. My once-assured future was no more, but I had a job to complete. My assumption going forward was to serve until the Governor retired from office. I had no plans beyond that.

During Governor Burns' third term, the University of Hawai'i asked me to return to serve as Vice President for Business. The UH was having management problems and needed help, but I had no interest in that job. I discussed the request with the Governor; his advice was not to accept. I declined, but after awhile, they asked again; the UH was apparently in desperate straits. The DOT was in good hands with three capable deputy directors and experienced division heads. I loved the UH and decided to help, if I could. I saw it as a short-term assignment, a trouble-shooter role, a dead-end. This time, the Governor allowed me to resign, without comment.

The Governor was slated to retire in two years. A few months after I moved to the University, Governor Burns was diagnosed with terminal cancer and asked Lieutenant Governor George Ariyoshi to serve as Acting Governor. Governor Burns never returned to his office. I would never have left my post had I known that he would become ill. But it was too late; there was nothing I could do to reverse course.

Then, a short time later, University of Hawai'i President Harlan Cleveland announced his resignation and the Board of Regents began a national search to find his replacement.

University Management

I was nominated for the position of UH President, but because of my lack of experience in top management of a university, coupled with a decade of absence from academia, I hesitated to accept the nomination. I had never aspired to be University President. I finally gave in to the pressure from UH colleagues to provide for a larger pool of local candidates, if nothing else. My qualifications for the presidency were thin. My good friend Dick Kosaki, a McKinley classmate, had a long record of distinguished service at UH-Mānoa and would have been an excellent President. I assumed excellent candidates would apply from Mainland institutions, as well.

The University of Hawai'i system represented a unique and intriguing challenge. It was the only statewide university system in the country that also included community colleges under one governing board. When the dust settled, the Board of Regents had chosen me as the ninth President of the University of Hawai'i system.

It was not a universally applauded choice, especially within UH-Mānoa, our oldest, largest, and only graduate and research campus. I was surprised to learn that many saw me as a political appointee of the Governor, the kiss of death for academic purists. I had always thought of myself as an academic on leave and hoped, someday, to return to teaching and doing research. I was sure that I would be able to dispel the notion held by those faculty members who only knew me through news articles in which I appeared embroiled in some public controversy on State transportation matters, always political in nature. I was willing to be judged by my actions and made no special attempts to rectify the problem.

I might have been infected by Jack Burns' stoicism. Once, when he was being criticized from all quarters about an action he had taken, I remember asking him. "Governor, why don't you set these guys straight?" He replied, without any rancor, "A thousand angels dancing on the head of a pin, swearing I was right won't make me right. Only the result can show that." Then he went back to his paperwork.

Like Dick Kosaki, Hawai'i was home for me, and I was fully committed to spending the rest of my life here. Most presidents from out of state, with the exception of David McClain and Tom Hamilton, one of our greatest recent presidents, returned to their homes on the Mainland when they resigned. That's natural, and I do not fault them for doing that; rather, it is to be expected. Professional pride and personal integrity compel any president to do his or her best, but serving *your* university and *your* state is also a matter of the heart.

Many good things happened during my ten-year watch as President of the UH system, but most of the credit must go to the faculty and staff and their academic deans and directors of research institutes, the prime movers of all universities. The several Deans of the Colleges of Arts and Sciences, Ralph Hook and Dave Heenan of the College of Business Administration, John Shupe and Paul Yuen of the College of Engineering, Hugh Everly of the College of Education, Ned Kefford and Chauncey Ching of Tropical Agriculture and Human Resources, George Woollard of the Institute of Geophysics, John Jeffries of the Institute for Astronomy, John Craven of the Natural Energy Laboratory and the Law of the Sea Institute, Pat Takahashi of the Hawai'i Natural Energy Institute, Professor Ryuzo Yanagimachi of the Genetics Institute, Vince Peterson of the Neutrino Project, to mention only a few, were instrumental in building the faculty and programs of their respective colleges and laboratories. The law and medical schools were started in previous administrations and were just coming to fruition. Hilo College Chancellor Ed Mo'okini and West O'ahu College Chancellor Ralph Miwa did outstanding work. Vice President Dick Kosaki, followed by Chancellors Dewey Kim and Joyce Tsunoda, developed the seven two-year community colleges from concept to about half of the total system in terms of student count, dispersed over the four populated islands of the State. The community colleges have a distinct mission and a special faculty and is the fastest growing part of the UH system.

Before returning to Hawai'i, I had spent eight years at three excellent universities, Rose Polytechnic (since renamed Rose-Hulman Institute of Technology), MIT and the University of Illinois at Urbana, and had been trained by some of the world's best professors and mentors. I felt I knew a good university when I worked in one. The president plays a crucial role in guarding the quality and integrity of the university, but rarely deserves the credit and accolades he or she receives from the public for academic, research and student achievements. Those belong to the faculty, broadly defined. They build and define the university's quality. When things go awry, the president must be the chief defender of the university and accept full responsibility to set things right.

After retiring as UH President, I served for another ten years as the Executive Director of the Research Corporation of the University of Hawai'i (RCUH), providing management support and assisting extramurally funded UH researchers and projects. RCUH helped researchers navigate the many complex bureaucratic labyrinths that hamper their work. It was a pleasure to work with young, productive researchers doing the exciting work of discovery at a university under capable senior researchers and program directors.

Gratitude

The most important person who helped to shape my adult life I have left to the end — my wife Amy. Family came first for her. From the time our first child was born in Boston, taking care of the children was her top priority. The family grew to six children, and that meant she had very little time for the social life that other young mothers enjoyed. She always found a way to manage. She had no hired help; we couldn't afford it, except when I was UH President and a maid came with the President's residence. But the family was always Amy's personal responsibility. The kids were always healthy, clean, well-dressed and well-mannered. They could all read by the time they started school, and did well in school. Being kids, they did get into trouble, but she guided them through the difficult teenage years. In their critical growing years, I was often away. She was teacher, counselor, disciplinarian, nurse and chief storyteller at bedtime, then chief proctor when homework had to be done. That was when she was not being housekeeper, cook, seamstress, chauffeur. I did what I could to help, but she could not rely on me. Today we have a wonderful, close family, and most of the credit belongs to Amy.

I had the propensity for choosing jobs that often did not pay well, and the good fortune and luxury of being able to do them because she made it work. She always supported my career moves, even when it meant that the family income would suffer. The kids never felt deprived; they learned to share and help. They had to. Of course, they had their share of teen and other growing-up problems, but Amy managed them all. I was oblivious to most of them because she dealt with them so well.

The kids, now in their fifties and sixties, still call her often — the daughters several times a week, and the grandkids, as well. The typical telephone conversation at our home when I answer the phone goes, "Oh, Hi Dad. Is Mom home?" The family is the center of my life, and I know who the center of the family is — we all do, and are grateful for the time, love, wisdom, energy, care and laughter she gave to all of us. And, yes, discipline when they needed it. I was more of a problem, I'm afraid. We can all say to her over and over again, "*Okagesama de.*"

Conclusion

I am afraid I have exhausted the space allowed me in this essay, so I can only give one example of a highly complex organizational and planning problem that involved the travel industry. I have chosen this example — financing expansion of Hawai'i's airport system — to illustrate how one's values and attitudes can affect the outcome of some knotty problems. From it, I learned that not every problem can be solved, and a lack of preconceived (in other words, textbook) solutions may be an advantage in stimulating original thinking. This was the situation:

The airport system was required by State law to be self-financing; we needed to generate whatever funds we needed to build and operate the system. No State general funds (tax revenues) could be used. The post-statehood tourism boom required a plan for a new airport system. All overseas carriers, domestic and international, had to help finance airport developments on all major islands, even if they did not directly fly to those islands. Their passengers, however, did, and were expected to do so in increasing numbers in the future. In essence, all overseas carriers would have to help finance all the airports in the State system, whether they used them directly or not.

Understandably, the airlines objected to the scheme. A negotiating committee was formed, consisting of representatives of all the airlines serving Hawai'i and key DOT officials, assisted by the deputy attorney general assigned to the DOT. I chaired the meetings. I was determined to keep the negotiations friendly, be patient and focus on the long-term goals and benefits, even though the cost effects would be immediate and the benefits would lag. It was a hard sell. I knew that they would have trouble with their headquarters, as Hawai'i would probably end up with one of the highest landing fees in the world.

It took three years to conclude the negotiations, with annual threats by the airlines to take us to court. They kept sending higher-level negotiators to deal with the "unreasonable Hawaiians." To their credit, they negotiated in good faith and we kept the proceedings friendly and rational. We had to develop trust, which took time. They finally accepted our premise — that we were partners, not adversaries; we were in this together.

They were right. Their fees jumped up to be the highest in the country — but only temporarily, because we were right, too. As Hawaiʻi tourism boomed, passenger and aircraft traffic multiplied, fees from airport concessionaires increased and the airline fees declined to reasonable levels. Neighbor island airport development was managed carefully, and each major island was able to receive direct flights from the Mainland and foreign airports, as well.

Being considerate of the other person's problems and striving for the common good worked. To paraphrase an old song I remember, "Things that my mother had taught me…" Patience, perseverance and goodwill helped.

Fujio Matsuda began a second life after retiring in 1984 as the University of Hawaiʻi's ninth President. He went on to lead the Research Corporation of the University of Hawaiʻi and then the Japan America Institute for Management Science. Matsuda has also served on numerous for-profit and not-for-profit boards, including that of the Pacific Buddhist Academy, the first Buddhist high school in the United States.

Matsuda enjoys poetry and music, sings in the Honpa Hongwanji Hawaii Betsuin choir, and translates the poems of Kaneko Misuzu and Aida Mitsuwo in his spare time. He also writes the 232nd Engineers (his original 442nd company) and Band Chapter column for the 442nd Veterans Club's *Go For Broke Bulletin*.

Additionally, Matsuda keeps up with advances in sustainable energy systems and makes conscious efforts to reduce global warming. A lifelong learner, he takes classes in Japanese calligraphy, Chinese history and photography. Matsuda is a believer in the Urasenke motto of "peace through a bowl of tea" and is a longtime practitioner of *chadō*, the way of tea, as a member of the Chado Urasenke Tankokai Hawaiʻi Association.

Matsuda has been recognized by many organizations and institutions: In 1986, he was inducted into the McKinley High School Hall of Honor, which recognizes alumni who have made significant contributions to the community. In 1985, several Hawai'i donors established Fujio Matsuda Technology Training and Education Centers at Windward Community College and Honolulu Community College.

Also in 1985, the Government of Japan presented Matsuda with The Order of the Sacred Treasure, Gold and Silver Star, for advancing friendship and goodwill between Hawai'i, the United States and Japan. Matsuda was recognized as a "Living Treasure of Hawai'i" in 2004 by the Honpa Hongwanji Mission of Hawaii. That same year, Sen Soshitsu, the Sixteenth Grand Tea Master, presented Matsuda the first Urasenke Way of Tea International Cultural Award in Kyōto, Japan.

Fujio and Amy Matsuda celebrated their 64th wedding anniversary in 2013. They are the parents of six adult children and eleven grandchildren and celebrated the birth of their first great-grandchild in the summer of 2013.

A LIFE WITH MEANING

Rose S. Nakamura

I was born Sadako Kiyosaki in Hilo. When I was little, everyone called me "Koko-*chan*." In fact, many of my relatives and close friends from Hilo still refer to me by that name. My father, Shizuo Kiyosaki, immigrated to Hawai'i from Hiroshima when he was about eight or nine years old; my mother, Masae Inouye Kiyosaki, was born on the Big Island of Hawai'i. Both my parents were bilingual.

I was the eldest of three children — all girls. I think my father wanted a son. He was really sports-minded, so he taught us how to ride a bicycle and how to play softball. Every Sunday, he would take me to the baseball games. When he grew older and joined the *Makule* League, I was recruited to play first base!

I went to Hilo Union, Hilo Intermediate and Hilo High School. Our high school class, the Class of 1946, celebrated more than sixty years since we graduated. A group of us still get together; in fact, we started a *tanomoshi* group.

My father was a cabinetmaker for American Factors. The warehouse where he worked was near Hilo Bay and only a block away from our house. Dad and his brother opened a store nearby on Kamehameha Avenue, so Dad left American Factors and together, he and Uncle worked full-time on the business. Later, they opened another business, which they called the Drive In Market, and closed the first store. The Drive In Market was the first modern-style supermarket in Hilo. I grew up helping with the family business.

Uncle's house and our house were next door to each other, and between our two houses was a *furoba* (traditional Japanese bath house) that our families shared. The children were responsible for building the fire to heat the water every day. On weekends, all of the cousins took turns doing the laundry. My cousin and I would team up so we could get the job done quickly. My uncle had eight daughters, so if you add my sisters and me, that totaled eleven girls — just like a football team!

My parents hired several young people to work in the store and they boarded at our house — we lived upstairs and they lived downstairs. My parents took care of them, too.

My mother worked in the store and my aunt looked after things at home. Every day, someone would come in to cook the families' dinners. All of the children ate with our grandfather, then the workers ate and, finally, my parents.

Our family was severely affected by the bombing of Pearl Harbor. On the evening of December 7, 1941, at about midnight, I heard someone knocking on my uncle's house. Uncle was immediately arrested and taken to the Volcano area, where he was held until he was transferred to a relocation camp on the Mainland. He was probably suspected of being disloyal to America because he traveled back and forth to Japan to purchase items for the store. My father just worked in the store, so he was not arrested.

After Uncle was taken away, there was no question of what would happen to his family. Dad said, "We will take care of everybody. No need to go to the Mainland." So we lived like one big family. We attended Japanese school until the seventh grade when the schools were closed because of the bombing.

Although food was rationed, we had a store, so we never worried about how we would feed everyone. My mother was small in stature, but she worked every day in the store. Uncle had a seven-seat Packard, so my mother would drive all of us girls to school. She wasn't afraid of anything; she would drive a jeep, even a truck. When we reached high school, though, we would walk to school with our friends.

Because of the war, I learned many valuable lessons about the importance of family, even our extended family of workers, and helping each other.

My father was the block warden during the war. Every night, he made his rounds of our neighborhood. Because of that, he knew which families were making do and which ones were in need, and, from his store, he helped people who didn't have food, especially rice. There were some families who couldn't even pay for food during that time. These things impacted me deeply.

One person who influenced me greatly was my grandfather. I have fond memories of Kiyosaki *Ojii-chan* eating dinner with us grandchildren every night. He would have his *sake* every evening before dinner and then we would all eat together. Our time with him was indeed precious. He would talk to us about how to behave, how to talk nicely to people and encourage us to eat our food, even if we didn't care for it. When *Ojii-chan* went out, even if only in the neighborhood or to downtown Hilo, he would always be neatly dressed, down to his hat. *Ojii-chan*'s room was in Uncle's house, so he was always close by. Even in his last years, we took care of him.

I was also deeply influenced by my ninth-grade English teacher, Miss Peace Tan. She was a pretty young woman. Miss Tan shopped at our store. One day, she convinced my father that we should all have English names. My father agreed, so all of us had our names legally changed to English names. I took the name Rose, and my sisters changed their names to Iris and Sarah. This was during the war and we were trying to become westernized and more "American."

We lived near the Hilo Hongwanji. The dormitory and school buildings were just beyond our backyard. I attended kindergarten, Japanese School and Sunday School all at Hilo Hongwanji. I was exposed to Buddhism from very early in my life. My father was active in temple activities and my uncle was on the board of Hilo Hongwanji. When I was in the sixth grade, I received a dictionary from the then-Bishop of Honpa Hongwanji, which I treasure to this day.

On April 1, 1946, during my senior year in high school, a massive *tsunami* hit the Big Island. In those days, there was no *tsunami* warning siren like there is today.

Our house was a two-story wooden structure, which was typical of the homes in that area. The workers lived downstairs and we lived upstairs. We had a *tansu* (Japanese-style chest of drawers) in which our nice *kimono* were stored. All of them were damaged when the water rose to about four feet high. Everyone in our family was safe, but all of the *kimono* were ruined.

Another *tsunami* hit Hilo in 1960. I was married by then and living near the University of Hawai'i's Hilo campus. By then, the *tsunami* warning system was in existence, so we told my parents to evacuate. They said that their neighbors were still there, so they were going to stay put, too.

When the wave hit, my parents were trapped in the house, hovering under the dining room table. My uncle escaped from one of the bedroom windows, but my aunt was trapped because the ceiling caved in on her. The destruction was horrific; there was so much to clean up. All of my sisters and cousins came from Honolulu to help, even with their young children in tow. Before they arrived, however, someone had to identify my aunt at the morgue. My only cousin in Hilo at the time just couldn't do it, so I said I would do it.

The sight of sixty dead bodies lying in the morgue was overwhelming and haunted me for many years. I couldn't recognize her face, but I did recognize her nightgown. I had to tell my cousin that I thought the woman was her mother. I was so haunted by the image that I couldn't talk about it for a long time. Now I can, because I understand the importance and fragility of life.

My parents moved in with us and we helped them find a new home after the State purchased the devastated area and declared it a *tsunami* zone.

Prior to resettling in Hilo, I had majored in health education and physical education at the University of Hawai'i. Our professors encouraged us to get hands-on experience, so I did a lot of volunteer work. Every week, I would go to Palama Settlement in Honolulu and work with the youngsters, mostly boys. Drawing on what I had learned in my younger days playing softball, I helped the kids improve their skills.

After I started helping out at Palama Settlement, the staff member I worked with accepted a directorship at the Waiakea Social Settlement in Hilo. One day, he called me and said, "Rose, can you come and join me? I want you to do some group work."

It was a wonderful opportunity to go back home to Hilo. As the eldest child in my family, I felt a responsibility to help my parents. Japanese call that *oyakōkō*.

While doing the group work at the Waiakea Settlement, I received a call from UH-Hilo. They were looking for a part-time instructor to teach some health and physical education classes. So, I talked to my boss, who said I could do my group work at night. Thus, I was able to juggle both a full-time and a part-time job. Of course, I was single at the time and that presented opportunities for me to gradually move into a full-time position at UH-Hilo.

I formed a softball team of high school girls called the Sharpettes. I wasn't their coach at the time, but I was thrilled when the team took the championship. I also formed a badminton team at Waiākea that competed in Nā'ālehu and at other places. Working with the parents and the younger ones was a way for me to give back to my hometown.

In time, I married Paul Nakamura, who, like me, was from Hilo. Paul was drafted when the Korean Conflict started. We were expecting our first child at the time, and I was working full-time at UH-Hilo. I gave birth while Paul was in Officer Candidate School at Fort Benning, Georgia. It was hard being separated, but we managed with the help of both our parents. Because of that experience, I know what it's like to be a single mom.

Our second son, Neil, was born at Fort Ord, California, where Paul was stationed for a year and a half. I had to resign from my UH-Hilo position during that time.

When we returned to Hawai'i, my husband taught at Hilo Intermediate School and also coached. I was fortunate to be able to return to my position at UH-Hilo due to someone going on maternity leave. In those days, teachers' pay was very small, so Paul joined the National Guard to earn extra income. When the Guard offered him a full-time job, he was conflicted, because he was just about to go into the Hawai'i Department of Education's administration program to become a school principal.

After a few years with the National Guard in Hilo and a great deal of thought, he decided to accept the offer and came out to Honolulu. He lived in the bachelors' quarters at Fort Ruger while I stayed behind in Hilo with our children. I wanted Paul Jr. and Neil to finish the school year and then move during the summer. Our daughter Gwen was only a year old at the time.

I was the Director of Student Personnel during my last four years at UH-Hilo, working with the students and teaching at the same time. When my husband accepted the position in Honolulu, I decided to focus my career on administration, so Mrs. Marion Saunders, whom I knew from UH-Hilo, arranged an interview for me in Honolulu, and I was hired as a program officer for the East-West Center.

Paul's new job with the Hawai'i National Guard meant he was away for two weeks every year, attending summer camp. We didn't see him at all during those times. With three young children in a new home and a different environment, it was hard not having him with us. We were also separated on weekends when he had duty or drills. My husband made the National Guard his career and retired as Chief of Staff.

There is a nine-year difference in age between our second child, Neil, and our only daughter, Gwen. The boys were wonderful babysitters; they really looked out for their sister. They took her wherever they went, even on dates.

Both boys graduated from Kailua High School and received scholarships to UH. We attended all of their soccer games as a family. From our children, I learned that sports and music are good for learning discipline. My husband and the boys all played in the band when they were in school. Gwen, too, has always loved music.

She was eight years old when she started taking piano lessons. When the musical group, the Carpenters, came to town, the Hōkūlani Elementary School fourth grade class had a chance to sing with them. Gwen was in the sixth grade when Hōkūlani introduced instruments. She chose the clarinet, but at Jarrett Intermediate School, she switched to saxophone and was nurtured by her teacher there. At home, she would play the piano and the sax. Even though there's usually no seat for saxophone players, her teacher took her to play in the Junior Symphony. In high school, the band teacher worked closely with her. Gwen said her band teachers were like second fathers to her.

My husband and I noticed that Gwen would always express her feelings through music. I used to tell my husband, "You notice there is feeling in the way she is playing?"

Gwen loved music so much that she decided to pursue her Master's degree in music education. Immediately after receiving her degree, she got a call from Castle High School — their band teacher was pregnant and the band was scheduled to go to the Rose Bowl. They wanted Gwen to help prepare the band for its performance. She did it, and has devoted herself to teaching music ever since.

I supported our children in whatever they wanted to do. When the boys were playing soccer at UH, they would bring home the dirty uniforms of their teammates who were international students. They would say, "Yeah, yeah, my mother will wash it for you." And, Gwen would say, "Oh yeah, come over, my mother won't mind if you come."

I'm glad that my children made friends with students from all over the world, because I have always believed in the importance of bridging cultures and people. When I worked at UH-Hilo, I had the opportunity to demonstrate with Mrs. Saunders that a smaller campus was beneficial to international students.

During my nearly twenty-six years of working with international students at the East-West Center, I did informal counseling and fostered intercultural group activities. Some students were homesick, so I brought them to our house for some social activities.

During that time, one of the Center's presidents was having a difficult time relating to the students. Sometimes when you "talk down" to the students, they react to that. One president wanted only the "cream of the crop" as students. The students reacted to that, so the president asked me to help him talk to the students.

I said, "You're asking me?" Finally, I said to him, "If I can help, I would like to bring you to their terms." So I found a place for group meetings. Those were the days when computers were just being introduced and I was worried about the students' safety, as they walked between the dormitory and the UH computer labs. So, we got a computer lab installed in the dormitory. And, we did a lot of intercultural things so they would mix with other students and staff. Some of the students had a difficult time adjusting to life in Hawaiʻi or the academic programs. If they were having difficulty with English, I would go to bat and find someone who could edit their thesis. So, basically, I was an advocate for the students, working with them. Sometimes, we have to remind ourselves that the Western system of education can be very different from the educational system of other cultures, so we need to be understanding and empathetic.

I remember one incident involving a woman from Malaysia. On Fridays, the Center provided a shuttle to Star Market so the students could do their grocery shopping. One of the students was charged with shoplifting. They said she had not paid for something. She came to see me and explained what had happened. Realizing that she did not intend to shoplift, I asked the Vice President if we could get some legal advice for her. Eventually, the charges against her were dropped. All of this was well outside of my area of responsibility, but I felt I had to demonstrate faith and trust in her.

When I retired from the East-West Center in 1988, my husband encouraged me to do something I enjoy. I like to do things more at the grass roots level. That's me. For instance, there was an elderly woman who lived right across the street from our Project Dana office in Mōʻiliʻili, so, she was a neighbor. She called and asked if someone could take her to the telephone store to purchase a telephone with large numbers. I said, "Sure, I'll take you."

I think it's important to continue living and working with people. I'm a strong admirer of Catholic Charities and the work they have done. When I retired, one of the first things I did was study Japanese language. Then, people started asking me to serve on boards of directors. I turned them down.

Then, one day at church, my good friend Shimeji Kanazawa proposed a project that became Project Dana, a program founded on the Buddhist principle of *Dana*, or selfless giving. "OK, I'll help you," I told Shim. "Look at what Catholic Charities is doing. Maybe the Buddhist community can do something similar." Project Dana was established in 1989 and provides a variety of services to the frail elderly and disabled to ensure their well-being, independence and dignity in a place of their own choosing.

When I listen to the Buddhist teachings, I think of how important they are. We live in an interdependent world and we have to be friends.

For example, when I was first hired at UH-Hilo, the campus was at another location. They moved to the new campus during my second year there. I opened UH-Hilo's first dormitory. Later, a couple was hired to manage it. Completion of the dorm was behind schedule, so one of the students who had applied from Kona didn't have a place to stay for the three weeks until the dorm was finished. I told him that he could stay at our house. He eventually went on to get his doctorate. I had forgotten that he had roomed with us, but, amazingly, he never did. When I saw him years later, he said he would never forget that we let him stay at our house!

That taught me that we don't have to be alone in this world. All of these things I do out of love for people. Experiences of pain and suffering, like helping my mother and helping *Oba-chan* — they influence your outlook on life. Doing things from the heart is very important.

I have concluded that learning is a lifelong process. No matter where you are, it's important to keep learning and to keep facing challenges. When you look at the *tsunami* and what happened, it makes you realize that life is so precious, so we have to live life with meaning.

Rose S. Nakamura's retirement from the East-West Center opened the door to a new and fulfilling "career" as the volunteer Executive Director of Project Dana, the caregiving support program she and her longtime friend Shimeji Kanazawa co-founded at the Moiliili Hongwanji Mission. Based on the Buddhist precept of *Dana*, a Sanskrit term meaning "selfless giving," Project Dana is today an interfaith project involving more than seven hundred volunteers who assist over a thousand elders by providing home and telephone visits, respite care, family caregiver support, home safety assessments, transportation to and from medical appointments, grocery shopping, religious services, hospital and care home visits, minor home repairs and light housekeeping.

In 1993, Nakamura was presented the first "Rosalyn Carter Caregiving Award." She received Honolulu's first "Forever Young Award" in 2008, and, in 2009, the National AARP presented Nakamura with its "Inspire Award" in recognition of her compassionate caregiving. Nakamura was also named a "Living Treasure of Hawai'i" in 2000 by the Honpa Hongwanji Mission of Hawaii. She and her late husband Paul raised three children.

RUSTY'S GARDEN OF LOVE

Ted T. Tsukiyama

My dog Rusty was always part of our family.

Rusty was born on September 29, 1999; his mother was Nala, a boxer owned by my daughter Sandy. His father was a Rhodesian Ridgeback, a feral dog who lived in the nearby Woodlawn forest of Mānoa. Rusty was the only male in Nala's litter of six. Sandy wanted so badly to keep him, so a few months later, on my birthday, this cute puppy with a red ribbon tied around its neck was placed in my lap as my birthday present.

Rusty quickly grew into a big, strong, eighty-five-pound boxer-Ridgeback. After receiving puppy and adult obedience training, he became a socialized and well-adjusted dog who never bit anyone nor showed any aggression toward other animals or people. He was blessed with a calm and mild temperament and a poised, almost-dignified bearing and demeanor.

Rusty was not only smart; he was psychic and could read my mind. If I were just thinking of taking him for a walk, without my even saying a word, he would take one look at me and start yelping and prancing with joy. But on a warm, sunny afternoon, if I were thinking "bath," Rusty would pull a Houdini disappearing act and was nowhere to be found!

Rusty wasn't just a good pet and companion. He zealously performed his job as watchdog over our home and property and protector of our family, which always made us feel safe and secure.

Dogs are capable of showing unbounded love for their masters. Some people will remember that familiar street person and his little dog walking around the School Street area, scavenging for salvageable rubbish. That little terrier never left his side, never sniffed around like other dogs. He would stop every few steps and look up at his master with adoring eyes. That dog did not know or even care that his master was a crippled, homeless, dirty, penniless scavenger, totally ostracized and avoided by society, for here was the only person who fed and cared for him, and he, in turn, loved his master with all his heart. We humans could learn so much about what pure, boundless, unqualified love is all about from that little dog.

Likewise, all Rusty wanted out of life was to be near his master at all times. Wherever I went, he was my shadow. So, wherever dogs were allowed, I would take him along. He loved to ride in cars, so the front passenger seat of my car was reserved for Rusty whenever he rode with me on my errands. My wife Fuku had to ride in the back seat.

Rusty was, unquestionably, a member of our family, and we spent lots of good times together over the years.

But tragedy struck on December 15, 2007, when heavy winter rains resulted in a landslide in the rear of our property. Several tons of rock and debris came down the hill, burying Rusty, who happened to be walking by. A twelve-inch square strip of skin was ripped from his back and his lower spine was damaged. His left hind leg was also broken and he suffered other internal injuries. The veterinarian said she had never treated such a badly injured dog and that it was a miracle he survived. It would have been more merciful if we had put him to sleep then, but we asked the doctor to try to save him.

It took Rusty six long, painful months to recover. He endured painkillers and medical care all that time. There were hospital visits and several operations, the last of which was the amputation of his fractured left leg, which refused to heal. We grew closer to Rusty as we nursed him, massaged him, took him for acupuncture and swim therapy and prepared special diets for him while he gradually regained his health.

One day in February 2009, he collapsed. He grew weak and his stomach became bloated. A medical scan showed that he had a cancerous tumor in his stomach that had hemorrhaged; the doctor said there was absolutely no hope of curing him. Our family gathered around to give Rusty our last hugs of farewell as the lethal injection was administered, sending him off to a final rest and eternal peace. I will always remember that day — it was February 14, Valentine's Day, the day of love.

One of the most famous monuments in all of Japan is the bronze statue of a dog that stands outside of Shibuya Station in Tōkyō. It was erected in honor of a dog named Hachi-ko, who won the hearts and admiration of the Japanese people, because every day at four o'clock in the afternoon, he would make his way to Shibuya Station to wait for his master, a university professor, to emerge from the train station. The two would then walk home together. One day while at work, the professor suffered a massive stroke and died, unbeknownst to Hachi-ko. The professor's widow eventually found a new home for Hachi-ko and moved away. But the loyal dog knew only one master and continued to go down to the station every day, faithfully waiting for the professor to come home. Some versions of the story say Hachi-ko himself died at the spot at Shibuya Station where he waited, every day, for his master.

Our home is built on a hillside overlooking the street. Rusty did not own a watch, nor did he know how to read time. But every day, at around five in the afternoon, he would take his place at the lookout point, his eyes fixed on the street below, waiting for me to come home. As I drove up the street, I could see his brown form rise up, his tail wagging wildly, yelping for joy as he welcomed me home.

After Rusty was gone, I planted a flower garden at the lookout point in his memory and sprinkled his ashes over the flower garden. A rose bush now grows in the exact spot where Rusty waited for me. It produces bloom after bloom of big, beautiful, pink roses that lean toward the street. Surely, Rusty is still there, and with each lovely bloom that appears, he is telling us that he has not forgotten us and is thanking us for all the good times we spent together and sending us his undying love.

Ted Tsukiyama is a retired attorney and labor arbitrator who served in the Hawai'i Territorial Guard, the Varsity Victory Volunteers, the 442nd Regimental Combat Team and the Military Intelligence Service in World War II. Tsukiyama earned his law degree from Yale Law School in 1950 and was admitted to the Hawai'i Bar that year. Early in his legal career, he worked with attorney Masaji Marumoto, who was subsequently appointed a Hawai'i Supreme Court Justice.

Tsukiyama is a *bonsai* enthusiast and a dedicated researcher on Japanese American involvement in World War II. In 2001, he was presented The Order of the Rising Sun, Silver Rays, in recognition of his work in building goodwill between Japan and the United States and for his involvement in the World Bonsai

Friendship Federation. In 2003, Tsukiyama was recognized as a "Living Treasure of Hawai'i" by the Honpa Hongwanji Mission of Hawaii. The UH Founders Alumni Association presented its 2012 Lifetime Achievement Award to Tsukiyama in 2012. He and his wife Fuku are the parents of three adult children.

ALOHA AND 'OHANA:
AT THE CORE OF HUMANITY

Richard H. Kosaki

Education has been my life. Since entering the first grade at Waikīkī School in 1930, my life has been associated with education — as a student, professor and university administrator.

It all started with parents, who very much wanted their children to have a good education. My parents were immigrants from Japan and they instilled in us some cultural values that contributed to our success in school. These included: *giri* (duty, obligation), *doryoku* (to endeavor, to do one's best), *ganbare* (persistence) and *gaman* (to persevere, to endure).

One individual from Japanese folklore who personified these values was Ninomiya Kinjiro. My parents placed a little clay statue of Ninomiya Kinjiro in a prominent place in our home. He was a very poor lad who wanted so much to learn that he was always reading a book as he went about his daily chore of finding firewood in the forests to help his impoverished family. At night, because his home had no lights, he would read by moonlight or by the light of the fireflies. (Interestingly, during my 2004 trip to Japan, which included a visit to Kōchi, the birthplace of my parents, my sister asked me to purchase a statue of Kinjiro, presumably to encourage her grandchildren to study hard. I looked all over the city, but could not find Kinjiro's statue. In my visits to Los Angeles, I noticed that a large and prominent statue of Ninomiya Kinjiro graced a busy street corner in the Little Tokyo District.)

My parents' devotion to education was evident also in their purchase of the twenty-volume "The Book of Knowledge" when most of us were in grammar school. (By then, my parents had a limited knowledge of English.) Those volumes must have cost a lot and my hard-working parents were far from wealthy. Father worked most of his life as a waiter in the Waikīkī hotels, and Mother labored "24/7" with her home laundry business. (We lived in Waikīkī on the Diamond Head side of Paoakalani Avenue, which my University of Hawai'i sociology professor described in class as the "slum side.") We were not wealthy, materially, but we were not "poor" as defined by Michael Harrington in his landmark study of poverty in America. He defined poverty as a "lack of motivation." By his standards, we were "rich," as we were highly motivated.

I enjoyed going to school. I enjoyed my classmates and most of my teachers were good and caring. I did well in school with my parents, especially my mother, constantly looking after me and encouraging me. At Waikīkī Elementary School, Miss Rodenhurst, my third grade teacher, and Mrs. Lam, my sixth grade teacher, were especially helpful. At Washington Intermediate School, I was hired as a student worker in the school office, where the secretary, Mrs. Kishida, and the accountant, Mrs. Ebert, made me feel that school was my second home.

It was at McKinley High School that I became aware that education was much more than book learning. Our principal, Dr. Miles E. Cary, believed that the school experience is a real-life experience. If, as is commonly thought, school is a preparation for life, it can best be learned by making the school environment and experience reflect life in the "real world." Social studies should be concerned with the current problems facing our community and the world. We should learn to become responsible citizens of a democracy and we can best learn responsibility by assuming it now, in school. School thus becomes our community and we students should be primarily responsible for order in our campus community. Why not have student courts to judge fellow students for allegations of wrongdoing? Why not have a student government that collects its own fees, like taxes, and learns to spend it wisely for worthy student projects? Why not have a student government with popularly elected leaders and let them shoulder responsibility?

As student body president, I was privileged to be sent to Boston in the summer of 1941 to represent McKinley at the annual conference of the National Council of Student Body Presidents. I traveled alone. The trip was financed by the students, each of whom donated ten cents to watch the spring football game. The four hundred dollars I received was more than enough to cover all of my expenses. It was, of course, my first trip to the Mainland and it was an unforgettable experience. Back then, it took five days by ship and another five days by train to get to Boston. When I arrived there, I was interviewed as the delegate who had traveled the longest distance. When the interview began, the reporters looked a bit surprised and asked, "Where did you learn to speak English? You have a Boston accent!" It occurred to me then that many of my teachers in the public schools had come from the New England area, where most of the early Christian missionaries to Hawai'i had come from.

There were approximately two hundred student delegates and chaperones at the conference. I was able to mingle freely among the delegates, who wanted to know more about Hawai'i. At the conclusion of the conference, I was elected one of the vice presidents.

Principal Miles Cary continued to nourish our "little democracy" with his warm and caring personality. The McKinley High School of my day was the largest high school in what was then the Territory of Hawai'i. There were almost four thousand students in three grade levels — sophomore, junior and senior. Even with such a large student body, Dr. Cary managed to get around the campus and make the students feel that he personally cared for them. Years later, in an obituary on Dr. Cary, a former student reportedly said, "I was a nobody on campus, just the average student, but I always felt that Dr. Cary cared for me."

I was one of the fortunate ones who got to know Dr. Cary well, as I had an active role in student government as sophomore class president and student body president in my senior year. When I won the school's oratorical contest that year, Dr. Cary said to me, "I think you can write a better speech for the Territorial finals." He knew that I lived in a crowded home, so he offered to let me stay at his home for a couple of nights so I could revise my speech. I spent two nights in the cozy study of his comfortable home in Mānoa, where I was left alone to rewrite my speech.

Years later, I was most fortunate to be with Dr. and Mrs. Cary again when I did my graduate work at the University of Minnesota.

After leaving the principalship of McKinley, Dr. Cary had gone on to become a professor of education at the University of Minnesota. The two years we spent with him in Minnesota only reinforced my respect for his sterling qualities as a teacher and citizen.

Dr. Miles Cary was my first mentor. He taught me that schooling and teaching transcended book learning. He taught me that a school administrator and teacher must personally care for all his students and must treat each equally. He illustrated that one must be a responsible adult and that responsibility is best developed by having students actually shoulder responsibility while in school.

World War II began during my senior year in high school and disrupted my schooling. At the beginning of my sophomore year at the University of Hawaiʻi, I volunteered for the U.S. Army. I was inducted into the Army on January 3, 1944, and sent to Camp Savage, Minnesota, to train as a Japanese language specialist in the war against Japan. (Shortly after the war began, American citizens of Japanese ancestry had their draft status changed to "4C: Enemy Alien." This was later changed so we could enter the armed forces.)

I was placed in a six-month accelerated program at the Military Intelligence Service Language School at Camp Savage in Minnesota. Never had we studied so hard. Our unit consisted primarily of Japanese Americans, but there was a smaller unit consisting of white Americans who also were learning Japanese. Most of these soldiers had graduate degrees in foreign languages and seemed adept at learning languages. Every Wednesday afternoon, we held one-to-one conversations in Japanese with members of this group so they could become more skilled in hearing and speaking Japanese. Six months later, at our graduation ceremonies, which were held separately, they were awarded the rank of second lieutenant while we received the rank of corporal.

While there was obvious institutional racism in the armed forces, as we were serving in segregated units, I did not experience racism in my daily activities. This was most evident in my three months of training in Officer Candidate School at Fort Benning, Georgia. Although we Nisei soldiers could not be granted officer status by completing our language training, much later, we were given the opportunity to be selected to enter and to successfully complete four months of intensive training to become infantry officers.

The seventeen weeks of intensive training at Fort Benning were rigorous and not everyone was able to graduate. The candidates were from all over the country. As I recall, there were four Japanese Americans and one African American in our company of one hundred twenty soldiers. Except for my size — I was the smallest in the class — I was never discriminated against, except for sometimes being given the lighter assignments. Indeed, there were signs of discrimination, such as being assigned to the "enemy" detail. We all joked that I best resembled the enemy — so I would sit up in a tree and drop small bags of white flour on my fellow soldiers during night maneuvers in the woods.

After three years in the U.S. Army, I returned to the University of Hawaiʻi, where I found a number of outstanding new faculty members. Among them were Professors Harold McCarthy in Philosophy, Tom Murphy in History and Ed

Vinacke in Psychology. I was majoring in Government, later renamed "Political Science," and my advisor was Professor Allan F. Saunders.

Dr. Saunders was an unusual teacher. He taught in the way of Socrates. Instead of lecturing, he preferred to discuss issues with his students, drawing them out and challenging them. He was not an "easy" teacher; he forced you to think, and to think in unconventional ways.

His challenging of the "conventional" was also seen in his daily life. When he arrived on the University of Hawai'i campus, male faculty members wore the conventional coat and tie to classes. Dr. Saunders chose to wear aloha shirts, like most of the male college students. They were better suited to Hawai'i's climate and I suspect he thought this better conveyed his belief that we are all equal. The University president reprimanded him, but he persevered and today, most of the male faculty members wear aloha shirts on campus.

Dr. Saunders enjoyed meeting students outside of the formal classroom. His office door was always open and he spent a great deal of time counseling students. He read countless books — we were impressed with his wide knowledge of the classics and of books in his professional field. I once asked him if he could recommend a list of books that he considered basic to a learned man's library. Within days, he presented me with a full page of recommended authors and titles, single-spaced. I still have a worn copy of that list, although I still have not read many of those books.

His effectiveness as a teacher went far beyond the classroom. He held class seminars at his home, as his wife Marion had also befriended the students. Dr. Saunders' treatment of students as equal human beings endeared many to him. Long after graduation, students kept in close touch with him. Fittingly, the social sciences building on the University of Hawai'i's Mānoa campus is named after Allan and Marion Saunders.

Professor Saunders' friendship and counseling have had a profound influence on my life. I entered the University with the intention of becoming a lawyer, thus my major of Political Science. However, Dr. Saunders asked me to consider becoming a Political Science professor and I, having become increasingly fond of university life and its environment, decided to enter graduate school with the goal of becoming a university professor.

I enrolled at the University of Minnesota because I intended to specialize in the study of state and local governments. Dr. Saunders indicated that the leading authority in that field was a professor at Minnesota. However, once enrolled in a variety of courses, I was very much intrigued by a professor of political theory named Mulford Q. Sibley. He was tall and gangly and wore loose-fitting brown suits — and always a red tie.

My undergraduate classes with Professor Sibley were always crowded. I later learned that many of those in attendance were not officially enrolled in his class, but wanted to hear his lectures. Professor Sibley was a brilliant lecturer. His lectures were well-organized and his thoughts stimulating and insightful. His demeanor and style were so engaging that, even in very large classes, students felt free to interrupt him and ask questions. He was honest; he opened his classes by expressing his personal biases: "I am a pacifist and a socialist." But we saw no bias in his explanation of the philosophies of John Locke or Karl Marx. More than once, the students voted him "best professor."

Despite his popularity on campus, some factions in the community viewed his political stands as subversive and more than once, crosses were burned on his front lawn.

In switching my major to Political Theory, I was appointed Professor Sibley's graduate assistant. This enabled me to attend most of his classes and I was able to confirm that those in attendance far outnumbered the names on the official class roster. His exams were not the usual true-false "objective tests," but rather "take home" exams in which the student had to write two or three essays on topics that had been handed out early in the term. As graduate assistants, we did the initial reading of these papers. It was time-consuming, but helped us to develop our own thoughts on the subjects at hand.

My wife Mildred and I got to know the Sibleys outside of the classroom. We helped them organize groups of students, often from foreign countries, who were invited for dinner and socialization. Through these informal discussions, I learned that Professor Sibley had organized such a complete philosophy of life that his answers to different problems and questions had a consistency that was admirable. I saw this trait of consistency as I accompanied him on some of his lectures to different community groups throughout the state. I found that he was just as effective in community settings as he was in the classroom. On one occasion, we were skeptical when he was invited to address a miners group in northern Minnesota. They liked him so much that they invited him back to be the main speaker at their annual banquet.

Professor Sibley showed me by his example how a highly principled person lives a full life, with consistency and humility, and that your thoughts can be effectively expressed and transmitted in thoughtful and gentle ways. There is no need for animosity and acrimony.

Upon completing my graduate studies, I was fortunate to be hired by the University of Hawai'i to work half-time in two different departments: the Government Department and the Legislative Reference Bureau (LRB). The LRB provided research and bill-drafting services for the Territorial Legislature.

I had worked in the Legislative Reference Bureau during my senior year of college, so I was familiar with its operations. And, I knew its director, Dr. Norman Meller. I well remember Dr. Meller because, as a student, I went for my first job interview with him. I had just come from a meeting with the University president, who said he would vouch for me as a good worker. When I mentioned this to Dr. Meller, he quietly brushed this aside and discussed other pertinent matters with me.

This trait of not being influenced by extraneous outside pressures was one of Dr. Meller's trademarks in managing the Bureau's affairs. Dr. Meller saw to it that the Bureau's work was objective and free of political bias. But the quality I admired most in Dr. Meller was his devotion to his duties as a public servant. I had never seen anyone work as hard and as long with such devotion and allegiance. He was strict about getting reports out on time and about the spending of public funds. He was the only director I knew of who almost consistently tried to submit the following year's budget below his current budget; the common practice was to automatically increase it by three to five percent.

These strict standards did not adversely affect morale in the office. While strict with himself and the office, Dr. Meller's personal concern for his staff was manifested in several ways. He familiarized himself with the family matters of each employee and took an interest in the personal development of his staff members. He and his helpful wife hosted many get-togethers, and staff morale was high. Even after most of us, including Dr. Meller, had left the Bureau, former staff members held occasional get-togethers. Dr. Norman Meller was the ideal civil servant.

I eventually became a full-time member of the University of Hawai'i's Political Science Department. In 1962, when I became department Chairman and President of the Faculty Senate, the University was searching for a new President. The decision was made to hire Dr. Thomas H. Hamilton, then-President of the State University of New York. The New York system was probably ten times larger than Hawai'i's system.

As President of the Faculty Senate, I had numerous meetings with President Hamilton, who was a newcomer to Hawai'i. I found him to be most cordial and open, and he had a good sense of humor. The fact that he and I were both in Political Science may have drawn us closer together. He was fascinated by our mixture of cultures and wanted to know more about Hawai'i. President Hamilton was scheduled to speak at his Inauguration Convocation, so he decided to circulate his draft among several staff members for their comments. A week later, he called me into his office and said he appreciated my comments, and then said, "You were the honest one in telling me that some of my remarks were condescending." He then asked me if I would leave my department and the classroom and join his staff. Thus began my career in university administration. President Hamilton later added locals Richard Takasaki as Vice President for Administration and Kenneth Lau as his assistant.

Dr. Hamilton assumed the presidency of the University of Hawai'i at the right time. He was an experienced administrator who had big dreams for the University and went about realizing them with teamwork and in cooperative ways. He was very effective at establishing rapport with the community, especially its political and business leaders. While personally modest, he gave great speeches that he wrote himself, sprinkled with gentle humor, often self-effacing. He was accessible to faculty and students and treated his office staff with respect and empathy.

A valuable lesson I learned from President Hamilton was his view of administration and administrators. "Administrators are necessary, but not important," he said. "What's important is what takes place in the classrooms, the libraries and in the laboratories." Humility was a trait also shared by my other mentors.

Thus, I was fortunate to be guided throughout my educational career by outstanding mentors like Miles E. Cary, Allan F. Saunders, Mulford Q. Sibley, Norman Meller and Thomas H. Hamilton. By everyday example, they impressed upon me important life lessons that one learns outside of the classroom. They embodied some common values — many of these cultural values are actually *universal* values that are embedded in most cultures.

My mentors were men of integrity. They were principled men with firm character traits of honesty and trust. They were dedicated to their work — *giri*. They personified Khalil Gibran's description of work: "Work is love made visible." And, they willingly devoted time and effort to their endeavors — *doryoku*. In adversity, they persisted — *ganbare* — and were patient and persevered — *gaman*. They respected and cared for their fellow man.

Above all, equality was their creed. They treated each person equally. This important and fundamental value is especially evident in the Hawaiian culture and those of us who live in Hawai'i are fortunate to be exposed to and infected by it.

There is a beautiful episode of Hawaiian values influencing the lives of the immigrant Japanese in Hawai'i. In her 1982 book, "Ganbare: An Example of Japanese Spirit," Patsy Sumie Saiki describes the scene. In the middle of World War II, two men interned in a U.S. concentration camp have a conversation. Sakamaki is the first Japanese prisoner captured during the attack on Pearl Harbor. Furuya is an immigrant Japanese who has long lived in Hawai'i, but is declared "disloyal" and arbitrarily placed in a concentration camp with hundreds of other Japanese from Hawai'i. After being isolated while in Hawai'i, Sakamaki is allowed to mingle with the Hawai'i Japanese as they are transported to a Mainland concentration camp. He has been observing the behavior of the Hawai'i Japanese. The following conversation takes place:

Sakamaki: "You Americans are so lucky…"

Furuya: "Americans? We're not Americans. We often think we are, but during emergencies such as this, look what happened to us. We realize we're Japanese…"

Sakamaki: "Ah, but you have a Japanese face and name…but inside you're no longer Japanese. You have a different philosophy. For example, we in Japan don't feel much responsibility for others, although we're taught to fight and die for our country…. our country comes first — before ourselves, before our families…. But another way of looking at it is, these people are precious….and these people constitute our country…. I think that's what makes….America great. You care for each other. I see you sharing your sad moments, your happy moments. You almost live each other's lives…"

Furuya: "Perhaps it's the Hawaiian influence, more than the American influence…. In Hawai'i, there's something called 'ohana, or extended family. That's a large family relationship where members care and share with each other…."

Sakamaki: "*Ohana?*" In Japanese it means a flower! That relationship — of caring and sharing — is as beautiful as a flower."

There is no doubt that the dominant Hawaiian values of *aloha* and *'ohana* have had a profound and positive influence on our lives. They form the bedrock for equality.

Equality is important in education. John Gardner, architect of "The Great Society," put it best:

"Ultimately, education serves all of our purposes — liberty, justice and all our other aims — but the one it serves most directly is equality of opportunity. We promise such equality, and education is the instrument by which we hope to make good the promise. It is the high road of individual opportunity, the great avenue that all may travel."

However, an education that does not impart values is empty and can indeed be used against man's welfare. The world suffers more today from the lack of goodwill and compassion than it does from the lack of knowledge. We need to realize that education involves matters of the heart as well as of the brain.

Richard H. Kosaki joined the University of Hawai'i's administrative ranks during the tenure of President Thomas Hamilton and went on to hold numerous posts, including Vice President for Community Colleges, Vice Chancellor for Academic Affairs, Chancellor of West Oahu College (today's UH-West O'ahu) and Acting Chancellor for UH Mānoa. He also served as President of Tokai International University in Honolulu. Kosaki is credited with developing the University of Hawai'i's Community College system, which today serves approximately half of the entire UH student population. He also helped to establish the East-West Center.

Kosaki has received numerous awards, including the McKinley Distinguished Achievement Award, UH Regents' Medal, UH Distinguished Alumnus Award and the Allan F. Saunders Award for Community Service. Additionally, he was conferred an Honorary Doctor of Law degree from Tokai University of Japan.

In 2000, the Government of Japan recognized Kosaki's work in promoting educational exchanges between universities in Japan and the United States by awarding him The Order of the Sacred Treasure, Gold Rays with Neck Ribbon.

Kosaki and his wife, Mildred, an educator in her own right, are the parents of an adult son.

"TALKING VALUES" — THE JULY 6, 2012, ZADANKAI CONVERSATION

Discussants: U.S. Senator Daniel K. Inouye, Irene Hirano Inouye, former Governor George R. Ariyoshi, former Consul General of Japan Yoshihiko Kamo, Bishop Ryokan Ara, Dr. Fujio Matsuda, the Reverend Yoshiaki Fujitani and Ted T. Tsukiyama.

The following is the transcript of the Zadankai "talk story" conversation on "Nisei Values" that was held in the office of U.S. Senator Daniel K. Inouye in the Prince Kūhio Federal Building on July 6, 2012.

* * * * *

Rev. Fujitani: We'd like to keep this "conversation," of sorts, as informal as possible. The Japanese term is *zadankai* — you just sit and talk. We have more formal things prepared for the book. The discussion here will be added to that book as a "closing conversation."

Consul General Kamo has been very interested also, so he wanted to be here to listen and to ask questions. Both of them, Consul General and Bishop Ara, feel that there must be something unique that the *Nisei* generation has contributed to Hawai'i and so they'd like to listen to what we have to say and satisfy their curiosity, you might say.

Ara-Sensei (quoting from Bill Hosokawa's book in Japanese): "No group has won greater respect or a position of more solid achievement in this country than have the Americans of Japanese origin. Constituting less than half of one percent of the population, they provide today one Senator and two Congressmen in Washington and distinguished representatives in almost every major field of endeavor in our national life." — *Edwin O. Reischauer, then-Harvard Professor and former U.S. Ambassador to Japan, 1961–1966, in Bill Hosokawa's "Nisei: The Quiet Americans," published by William Morrow and Company, Inc., 1969.*

Rev. Fujitani: That's a translation of Bill Hosokawa's book, "Nisei: The Quiet Americans." In it, there are a lot of interesting things that I think Bishop Ara has wanted to pass on from the *Nisei* here. According to Bill, there is something unique about the *Nisei*, and that's what he would like to know. Ara-Sensei is asking us to *reveal*, you might say, some of these things that are there that are not quite apparent. We would like to have that discussion.

Senator Inouye, deferring: Since I'm new to this…

Fujio Matsuda: Well, I think that one of the purposes here is, it's a very rare occasion when we can talk with you directly, so we want your take on that.

Senator Inouye: Well, If I may preface this…I have done what I can to study the thought process of our *Nisei*, my generation, and I find that our parents — and our grandparents, especially — if you investigate deeply, had intended to return to Japan after fulfilling their labor contracts. This resulted in many different things. For example, the Chinese had very little intention of returning to China, so the Chinese bought a lot of property here. On the other hand, although the Japanese outnumbered all other ethnic groups, we bought very little real estate.

Secondly, in many ways, because of our grandparents, I think we were much more Japanese than the present-day men and women of our generation in Japan. For example, when I was a child of four, I can't forget this because my grandfather gave me two words. I didn't understand those words. It was in later years that I had someone translate them for me and then the importance became apparent. One was *gimu* (duty), and the other was *meiyo* (honor), and you can imagine, four years old — what am I supposed to think? Incidentally, I had that translated after the war, so those two words had no influence on my life up until that moment.

114

But, speaking of *meiyo*, on the morning of our first attack in Italy, I got our little squad together. I was the assistant squad leader then at nineteen years old, and I asked a very simple question: "All of us know this is our first battle. All of us know that someone's going to get hurt, or someone is going to die. May I inquire as to what you were thinking about last night as you went to bed?" And to my surprise, because I did not expect this, not one spoke of, "I hope I don't get hurt; I hope I don't get killed." Although each one said it differently, they all meant the same thing: "I hope I don't bring shame to the family. I hope I don't dishonor the country." Depending on the person, the message was the same. I must tell you, it made me extremely proud. Not one thought about himself, injury or death: They all thought about the family or the country, not to bring shame, not to bring dishonor.

There was another thing when I was a child. I'm the *chōnan* in the family, and for six generations, my father, grandfather, great-grandfather, great-great-grandfather and great-great-great-grandfather were the eldest, according to the *koseki tōhon*. And, as a result, my grandfather felt it was his duty or obligation to bring me up as a Japanese. At home, it was a conflict because here I had a mother who became an orphan at the age of four, was brought up by native Hawaiians for about a year and after that by the Methodist bishop, so her Japanese was limited and her ideals were different. But he insisted that the Inouye family was *samurai*, although I knew better than that — we were a bunch of farmers. But the first time I fell and hurt myself, like a young kid, I started crying because it was painful, and he said very seriously, in Japanese, "*Samurai* don't cry," and, strangely, it has affected me so much that I never cried when I was injured from then on. Somehow, pain was not important to me. I think I've talked enough.

Fujio Matsuda: No, that's very interesting. My upbringing was very different in the sense that my parents were both Japanese. *Very* Japanese. I was brought up with a very strong Japanese bias in terms of values and language. I learned English as a foreign language when I went to public school. Learned Pidgin English first, of course. But this idea of *haji* — don't bring shame on your family, on your race — was also very strong in my family. In those days, when you read the newspaper, talking about crime and whatnot, you seldom, if ever, saw a Japanese name. And when they saw a Japanese name reported in the paper as having committed a crime, the whole community felt shame. It wasn't: "Oh, that's somebody else…" It

115

was a Japanese! My parents used to tell me, "Don't you dare bring shame on your family." So it was a similar thing.

Governor, did you have that kind of experience, also?

Governor Ariyoshi: Yes, my parents were very protective of me, and so they had great control over me. Whenever I went anyplace, I had to let my mother know where I was going and, from there, if I was going someplace, I had to come back and let my mother know I was going to go someplace else. In that way, I think I was very much under the control of my parents and I think I learned a great deal of things that they were doing. The word *haji* was very important: "*Haji okosanai yo ni*" — "don't bring shame." I think the term, "*Shikata ga nai*" is very important — you do what you have to do, but there are some things you can't help and you don't stay set and upset about that. A word like *gaman* — very important — you gotta pitch in there, persevere; and the word that was taught to me that was very important was *okagesama de*. My parents always used to tell me that no matter how good you are, it is not possible to do things by yourself. You need to have a lot of other people helping you. So, they used to tell me, "Don't boast about what you are achieving; always acknowledge that there were many others who were helpful" — teachers who were not always there at the particular time, but teachers who were very helpful in training you, helping you get to the point you are. And so they told me that the word *okagesama de* was very important. When I became Lieutenant Governor, and then Governor, I used to think about *okagesama de* a great deal. Before that, I didn't hear that word too often, but I began to feel more and more people using the word, "*okagesama de.*"

I think also, to me, when you talk about these things, I think we're talking about, basically, values of our parents, the *Nikkeijin*, and I hope that we will be able to, if we put something together, be able to talk in terms of what we have learned, what we do and how it becomes very useful in our own lives. I think each of us, if we stop and think, must have done some things, and whatever you did must have been impacted by values that were taught by our parents.

Rev. Fujitani: Yes, the idea of *okagesama de* is gratitude, to be grateful of what others...

Governor Ariyoshi: Well, it's more than just gratitude; it's acknowledging that there were many other people who have helped to produce what you did.

Fujio Matsuda (agreeing): You know, that's quite in contrast with the American ideal of independence and doing things by yourself. I think that's very important, too, but whenever I hear the phrase, "self-made man," I think to myself because of the same things that I learned from my parents, I think that no one, unless he lived on a desert island alone, did everything by himself. There's a whole generation, and generations of culture and civilization, that came before us. We can't say, "I did it all myself, without any help," because, for example, all of us went to public school. If it weren't for public school, we wouldn't be where we are today. Especially the GI Bill made such a big difference to us and what we ended up doing. That's partly because of the service we each performed, but on the other hand, if the country didn't educate the veterans to become useful citizens, the postwar boom wouldn't have happened. I think for myself, at least, that there really is no "self-made man" — everybody has been helped along the way. I think that is an important cultural difference that…

Governor Ariyoshi: And I think if you're willing to acknowledge that other people helped you in achieving what you did, you find plenty more other people very willing and wanting to come and to help, also.

Fujio Matsuda: And, especially in a democracy, you cannot do it by one person. You gotta build a team and do it together.

Rev. Fujitani: When I was thinking about what to talk about today, I sort of recalled that when I was growing up, there were all kinds of people, like our principal at Ha'ikū School was Mr. Wade, but his nickname was "Hage," because he wore a wig. He was *haole*, from England, a British *haole*. He was married to a Portuguese lady, so Mrs. Wade was a first grade teacher. And I was thinking of my own mother, who was born in Japan, but she was brought up here, so she was like a *Nisei* and I'd be more like a *Sansei*, in effect. But she had many friends of different races and I think that we were exposed to that kind of multinational, multiracial, multireligious community, so I think that was one of the differences we saw in the Hawai'i experience and the Mainland one. Maybe Irene (Hirano Inouye) can tell us about how it was on the Mainland, but you remember that the 442nd Regimental Combat Team (RCT) guys couldn't get along with the Mainland, what do you call, *kotonks?* I don't know how that name came about. Maybe Senator, you can explain that (laughter), but there was that kind of conflict until we had a common experience, I think. Senator tells of going to an internment camp in Arkansas and witnessing the camp life, the prisoner of war-type experiences of their buddies from the Mainland, and so their attitude changed. In other words, we had different experiences, but here in Hawai'i, we were exposed to more opportunities to get to understand other people. So we had Filipino neighbors, for instance. Some Filipino kids used to come to our temple to participate in Buddhist activities — I know they were Catholics — but things like that. So, in other words, as a kid, we were exposed to different kinds of people and different experiences and I think that sort of molded us into a little different kind of people, you might say. And part of that, I think, is this feeling that, wow, isn't this wonderful that we've had this kind of experience. This is that feeling of gratitude.

Governor Ariyoshi: I tell people I'm not a plantation child, so I was not exposed to some of the prejudices and biases that existed on the plantation. Nobody was like a *luna* (overseer) when I was growing up, so as a child, I didn't have any biases. I felt free to play and get along, and even fight, with other people of different backgrounds, which was very different from what I found when I became an adult and saw the control of the "Big Five" (five large corporations that controlled life in Hawai'i: Alexander & Baldwin, Amfac, C. Brewer, Castle & Cooke and Theo H. Davies). But, growing up, we were not exposed to those kinds of concerns. I think people develop feelings because of their experiences, and, to me, the people on the Mainland, they had all these biases and prejudices against them that we did not experience here, the camps that they were put into. The local people, the 442nd RCT people, used to tell me when I was going over in the service in California — many of them were coming back and they were telling me how restaurants in California, you go there and try to eat, and even though you were wearing the uniform, they would tell you you're not welcome; you can't eat here. I think that kind of experience, we were not exposed to, so we had very different kinds of feelings. And when you get people who do those things to you, I think it kind of pushes you down and makes you unable to really open up, and I think that probably happened to many of the people on the Mainland who were forced to kind of restrain themselves and pull back because they were made to feel very uncomfortable. Fortunately, in Hawai'i, we didn't have that kind of experience, even though as I grew up, I began to look at the economy and look at jobs and began to become very concerned about the control that the Big Five had over the economy of Hawai'i. And I think that's what made us get involved in politics in the first instance in 1954.

Senator Inouye: If I may differ a little...in many ways, we were very subtly taught to be racist. This is a rather difficult thing for me to talk about. If you look at ourselves in our youth, can you think of ten men who married non-Japanese?

Fujio Matsuda: No. In our family, at least, it was unthinkable...

Senator Inouye: And it was also unthinkable for a "normal" Japanese to marry an Okinawan. I had one of my best friends in McCully commit suicide because his family told him, "You will not see that woman." She was "*eta.*" Secondly, I was brought up, was born across the street from the Pacific Club. The only way I could get in was to be a waiter. All of these clubs, whether it be the Elks, or VFW (Veterans of Foreign Wars), or the American Legion — think about the American Legion — they were not open to us. You had to join a post named after a Japanese, which to me was insulting. That's why I stayed out of the American Legion.

Governor Ariyoshi: About when was this, Dan?

Senator Inouye: This was right after the war.

Governor Ariyoshi: Right after the war?

Senator Inouye: Yup. And then the so-called "Super Group" of the American Legion, Japanese could not become a member.

Fujio Matsuda: Just like Big Five?

Senator Inouye: Yup. And so, there were a lot of things. When I came back to Hawai'i — I won't mention the restaurant because it's a national restaurant, very fine restaurant — but I've never been there since. I had a date with a guy from Kamehameha. He invited me to lunch. We were old buddies from before the war.

So I said, "Let's get together." He named the restaurant, see you there at a certain time. I walked in there with four rows of ribbons, a hook on my arm and captain's bars. They told me, "I'm sorry..." This is after the war.

Governor Ariyoshi: Here in Hawai'i?

Senator Inouye: In Hawai'i!

Governor Ariyoshi: Oh my...

Senator Inouye: I'll tell you where. I'll whisper in your ear (laughing). So, these things were all over the place. And when you come down to it, I had to go to one of the different islands and convince the parents of one of my buddies, because he married a *haole* girl, that she was a wonderful woman. In fact, might be too good for him, school education and all of that. My father, when he married my mother — my mother is from Hiroshima, nothing wrong with her. But she was an orphan, and in the Japanese culture, orphans are a little lower. And they (my grandparents) didn't go to his wedding, and my father was the eldest son.

My uncle fell in love with a beautiful woman who was one of the best educators in Hawai'i at that time, college degree and everything, but she was [considered] "*eta.*" But since I'm the eldest son, I told my grandmother, "You gotta go. This is your son, the youngest son of yours." And this was a Christian church on top of that. Finally, she said, "I'll go." She put on a funeral *kimono* — you know, not a festive one — and from the moment she walked through the gates of the church, she took out her *juzu* (prayer beads) and started praying, "*Namo amida butsu, namo amida butsu,*" all the way in and sat down praying, "*Namo amida butsu...*" throughout the whole minister's saying, "Dearly beloved..." "*Namo amida butsu, namo amida butsu, namo amida butsu...*"

Rev. Fujitani: I guess we also inherited the prejudices of our folks and grandfolks, no? We were exposed to things like that, too...

Fujio Matsuda: But you know, that wasn't unique to Japanese. My wife's brother married a Chinese girl, and that was okay with her (my wife's) father, but on her side, they cut her off and said, "We won't have anything to do with you." It was only after the grandchildren came, then they reconciled. So maybe it's more an Asian custom, the barriers…

Senator Inouye: The Chinese, who have done well, married Hawaiians…

Fujio Matsuda: Part of the question that was raised by Bishop Ara was the "revolution" of 1954, the election — what changed and why were the *Nisei* so active compared to other veterans who came back and went to college, bettered their education and whatnot. They all became productive citizens, but only in Hawai'i was there an impact beyond just individual betterment. They reformed an entire society and maybe because we were in an oligarchy, a plantation community, while the rest of the country had gone past that.

Senator Inouye: I suppose that these were not collective decisions, but individual ones. In my case, I felt that we paid a price; a lot of blood was shed, a lot of people died, and it would be criminal on our side to go home and go back to the plantation. We'd have just wasted our time and thrown away our blood. And then, on top of that, for some reason, we were not welcome. For example, I remember having gone through Joe Farrington, he was our first honorary member of the 442. And he had all of us, the chapter presidents and others — he stood up and gave a nice speech, and he said, "I noticed that very few of you are members of the Legion, American Legion. That's the national organization. They'd love to have you." He said, "I'd like to sign you up to the Joe Takata Post." So I stood up and said, "I'd like to join *your* post. The conversation ended, because he knew very well that his post would not accept me. When the message got down to the ranks, nobody wanted to join. Even if it's a Joe Takata Post — it's insulting. *(Note: Shigeo "Joe" Takata was the first AJA to be killed in action in World War II while serving in the 100th Infantry Battalion.)*

Rev. Fujitani: Yes, we all had various experiences. By the way, Governor, I knew your dad — he was a *sumotori*. Yes, a very famous one.

Governor Ariyoshi affirms.

Senator Inouye: Really?

Governor Ariyoshi affirms.

Senator Inouye (laughing): How come you're not big?!

Rev. Fujitani: We haven't heard from Ted (Tsukiyama) at all.

Governor Ariyoshi: Before we continue, I want to respond to the question about how the *Nisei* got involved — for me, I think it's very important: Jack Burns (Hawai'i Governor John A. Burns, who served from 1962 to 1974). If it had not been for Jack Burns, in the 1954 election, I would not have gotten involved. He was the one who questioned me about my life as a child, and prejudice — and I told him I did not live on the plantation so I'm not familiar with the prejudice that you folks talk about. He told me, "OK, how about now, now that you're working?" I told him that I am enjoying starting off my law practice. I made a decision when I was in the eighth grade that I was going to become a lawyer, so becoming a lawyer was very important to me. He (Burns) was the one who convinced me that I had to get involved, and he talked about the Big Five and Tom Ebesu. So I think individuals play a vital role, and Jack Burns, at least in my case and in the case of many others he recruited to run, encouraged me to run in 1954. Had it not been for that meeting with Jack Burns, I doubt that I would have ever gotten involved in politics.

Rev. Fujitani: Out of the five of us, sort of, guests, here, I think four of us went to McKinley. But there's one who went to a private school; I think it's a private school — Ted. Ted went to Roosevelt (laughter).

Governor Ariyoshi: That's because he spoke good English. (more laughter)

Rev. Fujitani: Ali'iōlani Elementary, Lincoln Elementary, Kapālama Elementary, Jefferson Elementary, and Roosevelt High School were English Standard schools (for students who passed a written and oral test in English proficiency).

Senator Inouye: And, Stevenson Intermediate.

Ted Tsukiyama (laughing): They were public schools.

Rev. Fujitani: Yeah, there were some difficulties that we had gone through, but these are all behind us now. And I think Bishop Ara has been thinking that the

Nisei contributed to the building of a more stable society, but the *Sansei* have not had this kind of experience, so they are forgetting some of the values that the *Nisei* were brought up on…like *gambatte* (perseverance), and *oyakōkō* (filial piety), maybe…you know, these values that were important. So, this is what has to be perpetuated, according to Bishop Ara's point of view.

Governor Ariyoshi: I hope that in the process, this will not just be a story or statement of the values of the *Nisei*, but maybe how those values had an impact on the work that we did, to indicate that it's not isolated. The values have a great impact on what we do and how we go about doing things. And, success, in many ways, depends on and made a difference because of our own values. I'll give you a specific example. I am very troubled by the fact that we had furloughs and pay cuts made at the state level. I never had that because I asked for help, because I knew that in order to do things, I had to get the help of many people, and I asked for the help of the government employees. Nobody went to the teachers to ask the teachers for help when they were having these difficulties. Nobody asked them whether or not they could maybe take one or two more students in a class, and that could have avoided the need for public school student furloughs (in 2009). But it was people going ahead and doing things, and I think our values would have played a very important role in how you go about solving difficulties and trying to get people to help.

Senator Inouye: Well, the union movement did something. My father worked for Theo H. Davies & Company, a Big Five company. Union wanted to come in to organize, organize. And he (father) was the senior Japanese there, and he said, "No. No. No"…until Davies brought in a young *haole* kid, a Yale graduate, and put him above him. He (Senator's father) called the union organizer and said, "Come on over, sign us up. If that's the way they're going to play the game…"

Governor Ariyoshi: That's like Bert Kobayashi, who was working for Lewers & Cooke. And as competent a person as he is, he got up to a certain level, but then he could not go any further — everybody coming above him was a different color. That's when Bert decided he wanted to leave and become a lawyer, went to law school.

Fujio Matsuda: And if you look at it now, that barrier is gone. The *Nikkei* … in fact, many of the Big Five are no longer here…but they (*Nikkei*) broke that barrier and they were into all the Big Five companies. A *Nikkei*, Jeff Watanabe, is chairman of the board of Hawaiian Electric Industries, and Connie Lau, a Chinese American woman, is the president and CEO. *Nikkei* play key roles on the board of directors, or as officers of many companies in Hawaiʻi. So I think that brings us back to the question: How did our society change from the very tightly controlled oligarchy, where immigrants could not get past a certain level no matter how good you were? You had to train the guys who were brought in so they can do the job. I think the *Nisei*, in their behavior and performance during World War II, really changed two things: one, their own perception of what they can do, and second, the perception of the others who still resisted this — they wanted to go back to the old system, naturally, because they controlled everything. But to break that barrier down, I guess it required political action, because you can't just do it internally. But through Jack Burns and the 1954 election, that was changed.

Senator Inouye: That was just one step…I remember when I was in the Congress — this was the Congress, now — I was approached by Bill Norwood, who was a good friend of mine. And he said, "Five of us have gotten together — we put up enough money for you to become a member of the Pacific Club and for your dues for the next five years. How about you put your name up?" I said, "They don't want me; I don't want to join them." You know, here was a club where, supposedly, business people who have done well become members.

Fujio Matsuda: But then Governor Burns said, "Nope." The Governor was invited, but he said "no" for that very reason.

(Ariyoshi and Inouye agree.)

Governor Ariyoshi: I think part of it is, nobody really tried to teach the people who were doing this, somebody did it and this generation — it just keeps on going. But with the 1954 election, when the Democrats took over, we started talking about fairness in the community. I found there were many people in the Big Five — people like [Amfac President and CEO] Harold Eichelberger, Henry Walker, Boyd MacNaughton — they were very fair. I think they learned it was their discriminatory backgrounds — it was because that's what they did and everybody practiced the same thing. But I think we have to acknowledge that there were individuals who were very good people, fair people, and they only needed to be told that those practices had to change.

Fujio Matsuda (agreeing): That's true, but on the other hand, if you look at what's happening today with corporate power really exerting so much influence on our government…That's because the people with the power, they don't want to give it up. I don't know, but my feeling is here were the people, they're running Hawai'i the way they want it, and when you open the door and let the immigrants come in, they lose control. Even though, personally, they may not have really done that, at the minimum, they acquiesced in that system, so that's what keeps the system going when people just let it happen. But something had to jolt them out of that, and the question is, without the *Nisei* coming back to do that, would it have happened? Maybe not.

Senator Inouye: Well, our neighbors could not close their eyes to the fact that there were many examples of what happened in the war. For example, there's an organization called DAV — Disabled American Veterans — and you had to be injured to become a member. When the war ended, there was one DAV unit in Hawai'i made up of twelve members — twelve *haole* guys — and within a year, we must have had a dozen chapters, primarily Japanese because we were the only ones wounded. Right? Oh, there were others, but they were small in number. It became so obvious, for example, a Purple Heart organization and they felt so bad, they put a *haole* guy as president, because you know you can't have all Japanese, but about seventy percent of the members were Japanese. However, that military involvement has not gone beyond World War II and Korea. When Vietnam came along, they became very American. They stayed out. Same thing today — very small number of *Nikkei* volunteers; very, very small numbers.

Fujio Matsuda (agreeing): Well, I think that during World War II, the 442nd was a very identifiable group. Now if you join, you're all dispersed. I guess it's inevitable that the Japanese values would be diluted, if nothing else, because of interracial marriages among the descendants.

Senator Inouye: I did some studying of these things; I guess political [types] study these things. In my generation, I think less than five percent of our people got married outside of the group; now, this present generation, it's over fifty percent — that's a big difference!

Fujio Matsuda (agreeing): To give a personal example, my grandkids, two-thirds are *hapa* (mixed race).

Senator Inouye: My son is married to an Irish German — my only son.

Fujio Matsuda: So how do the Japanese values transmit to an Irish German Japanese kid living in Washington, D.C.? (Laughter) That dilution is going to take place over generations, but I think the important thing is that some of these Japanese values are important as *human values*, not as Hawai'i Japanese, or Mainland Japanese, but purely on the basis of one person to the next. The Japanese value of *omoiyari*, for example, being considerate of others, instead of "me first" or "me only" — that would benefit anyone in any situation. Society would be better if people were like that, instead of "me only." So I think these kinds of values, if we can preserve and propagate them, will build better societies, not just here in Hawai'i or the U.S., but between us and the Palestinians, or whatever. If we understand that we are all human beings and we can treat each other as human beings, like family, to me, those are the Japanese values that I learned. And through interracial marriage, the family transcends racial barriers.

Governor Ariyoshi: So we are not talking about Japanese values, perpetuating that for Japanese only...

Fujio Matsuda: No, no...

Governor Ariyoshi: But the values we have can be of great value to any person, no matter what the background might be. I think that's what we want to teach about the values of the Japanese — why, how they can be very valuable to other people, too, irrespective of where they are...

Fujio Matsuda (agreeing): That's right. Unless they're shared, they are going to be wiped out, anyway, when you get so many races and cultures mixed up. Hawai'i may be leading the country in blurring ethnic boundaries and that may be a good way to get rid of some of these prejudices and animosities that exist across ethnic lines.

Senator Inouye: We who serve in Washington have concluded that racism is alive and doing extremely well.

Rev. Fujitani: Consul General — do you have any questions to ask these gentlemen?

Consul General Kamo: Thank you for your invitation. It's very interesting, of course, to observe the discussions that are underway and some interesting discoveries of differences between Hawai'i and the Mainland. This is something that, among Japanese Americans, I never imagined or was familiarized with. Also, it seems that the discussion is now emerging into the point that Japanese values, some of them, could be very universal — to be good, kind of, for all humanity. So I don't know if these values are uniquely Japanese, or whether any other cultures have the same, or civilizations have the same values as the ones that we've talked about. Perhaps so, and I think that these values are certainly very valuable and very important for anybody to lead the country or better their lives and more, successfully. So, there's a concern that these values are now being kind of diluted, or fading away, so that future Japanese Americans should be given a chance to be exposed to these values and then to get immersed in these values for the betterment of their life. That's also very pertinent to the Japanese in Japan as well, because we Japanese in Japan, everything is so natural and heaven-sent, so we didn't have to think of the values that we were brought up with or inherited from our society, or from our value system, from our parents. We were born in Japan and that is really a decisive factor as to what kind of identity we have as a Japanese, because if we're born in Japan, that's a Japanese — speaks the same language and then observes, or enjoys, the same culture. These are all very natural things that we don't have to bother. What kind of other options do we have than to be a Japanese, but everything comes so natural. So, like *okagesama de, omoiyari* and lots of nice, important values that were discussed, I think really played an important historical role in Hawai'i. I think in Japan, they are playing important roles, but nobody, I think, is intentionally, or expressly aware that these are the ones that we are looking for, or we are looking to when we are in trouble or in difficulty. So, that's interesting . . . because maybe here in Hawai'i, even Hawai'i as part of the United States, you need kind of a self-identity to consolidate yourself, perhaps. But in Japan, as I said, we don't have to look for our self-identity, because there, it's just kind of very naturally . . . it's automatically a given, so in that sense, we are so ingrained — so not aware of these things, the importance of the search for ourselves, etc. And, that's why we can say that now our young people, including myself, maybe our generation is just using all these important values, or putting them into practice in our daily lives, but at the same time we know that this culture and these values are ingrained in us. So even though they are hidden in ourselves, or we may not apply them to some particular occasion, we feel that we are still deeply Japanese. Sorry, I have spoken too much.

Reverend Fujitani: Maybe that's exactly the way it was here in Hawai'i, too, as the *Issei* and the *Nisei* were trying to make a living, you know. There were a lot of values that they were born with and they didn't question. And now that we've seen the value of these, the question is, how do we retain them? How can we perpetuate them? I think that is the question that Ara-Sensei is asking. These have been valuable for the people here; how do we continue to have them?

Fujio Matsuda: I guess that as Japanese values — when being Japanese is hard to define, because we will all be only part-Japanese and part-Hawaiian or part-something else, eventually — what's going to be left is the universal values and what we call "Japanese" values must also be part of other cultural values, if they survive the generations. Most values have their origins in religious beliefs, so I think in the U.S., which is basically a country of immigrants where we have all of these different cultures and religions coming in, there are, you might say, competing values, or values that are perceived as different. Traditional Japanese values are basically Buddhist, Confucian, Taoist and Shintō — an amalgam of all of these built over thousands of years, so they're homogeneous. But the U.S. is such a young country that we're still going through the process. Our culture is cooking, with clumps of immigrant cultures. New ingredients are constantly being added. We're still identified as second-, third-, fourth-generation Japanese or Chinese, or Korean, Filipino, etc. Yet, we're all Hawaiians and Americans. Through many ethnic ways we relate to each other — through *"portagee"* jokes and *"pake"* jokes, eating Chinese food on Chinese New Year's, Thanksgiving turkey dinner with pumpkin pie, hamburgers and hot dogs on July 4th, King Kamehameha Day parades, World Series and Rose Bowl; everybody enjoys the Merrie Monarch Hula Festival and summer *obon* dances. These are occasions of shared values when we are one.

Governor Ariyoshi: Well, Fuj, I think you just described what Hawai'i is all about. We have people with different values; they come together, they work together, they don't do something against somebody else just because their values are different. I hope when Ara-Sensei puts the book together, it will be an acknowledgment of our values, but not to say that our values are better than someone else's values, but how our values affected us and made it possible for us to do the things we did, but not that it was better than somebody else's.

Ted Tsukiyama: Bishop Ara is nudging me to say something. Well, first of all, I really believe that what he's urging is a significant and important project, maybe because from his outside eyes he can see that these values characterize the *Nisei* and that they really affected the *Nisei* in their life and in their service and in their contributions to the community. He feels that is something that should be passed on, and getting firsthand sharing of these values, these traits, from the *Nisei* themselves is very important. You know, after all, we're a vanishing resource and I think it's valuable to get it firsthand from the *Nisei* themselves. So, there's sort of an urgency to what he's proposing and this is just the kind of thing that should start it off. I also share his concern that these values should be shared and passed on. I think that's the second part of our concern and endeavor.

For instance, this book here, "Japanese Eyes, American Heart," Bishop Ara and I are on the committee that published this book; there's a Volume Two that we're trying to get published (Volume Two was published in December 2012). This is not just the *Nisei* veterans' experiences and perspectives, but *Nisei* as a whole. There's a cross-section of *Nisei* stories — not so much veterans, but just civilians and women, especially women. We want to show how the Japanese, being a race that was targeted and under the gun, still managed to serve and fight and survive World War II, notwithstanding the general fear and distrust that was shown against the Japanese before the war and especially during the war. There's also a University of Hawai'i Colleges of Arts and Sciences project; it's called, "Universal Values For a Democratic Society — Nisei Veterans Endowed Forum Series." I think that project, too, recognizes the value of these values and that they should be passed on, not necessarily to the Japanese successive generations, but to all generations. While the *katchikan* — the Japanese word for "values" — may describe a certain set of values, like the stone monuments that are preserved over at the Japanese Cultural Center of Hawai'i, it's a real great thing, but it's needed, something that should be passed on and shared, and we should do all we can to help in that endeavor.

I heard a story about a Japanese tourist who went over to the Japanese Cultural Center and saw all these monuments with words like *kansha*, *chūgi* and *sekinin* and all these things, and she was looking at them with tears running down her face because she said, "You know, we don't have these things in Japan, anymore." So, actually, maybe Hawai'i is doing something, or at least is on the path to doing something to preserve, to share and to pass on these values. I'm all for anything that furthers that end, because as I say, it has to come from a resource that's vanishing. I think it is incumbent upon us *Nisei* that are still surviving to contribute to that. I think it's very worthy. What I'd like to say, though, is that this isn't just the *Hawai'i Nisei's* values, but the *Nisei* generation's values — broader perspective — and that's why I think we ought to hear from Irene (Hirano Inouye) as to what she'd like to say.

Senator Inouye: You know, what Ted brought up is very important, about passing it on. I noticed that past generations of Japanese — my grandfather, for example — had no hesitation telling me about his exploits, the exploits of the family, the role they played in the Russian War and all that.

One of the most common occurrences among 442nd families is that somebody comes up and says, "My father never told me about his involvement." Very few of us, for some reason, found it necessary, or desirable, to tell our sons and daughters what we did. I've never sat down with my son, but he didn't have to, because there were so many things written. But when you come down to it, all these songs remind you…Japanese songs about the wars and what they did during the war, and my grandfather was not gun-shy at all. But in my generation, we're not talking to our kids. Why? I don't know. We have nothing to be embarrassed about.

Reverend Fujitani: Well, it's claimed to be modesty, or might be false modesty…

Senator Inouye: I've had children come up to me and say, "Oh, my god, I didn't know you did that." But it's a common thing; I hear it all the time.

Irene Hirano Inouye: So I would agree with you, Ted, and say that the *Issei* and *Nisei* had values that transcended whether you grew up in Hawai'i or on the Mainland. The experiences of people who grew up in Hawai'i, as compared to the Mainland, were very different. As George [Ariyoshi] said, the discrimination was felt greater on the Mainland. Although there was discrimination in Hawai'i, it was much greater on the Mainland. This probably affected the self-confidence that *Sansei* or *Yonsei* felt about whether they could move into leadership positions.

You see far fewer Japanese Americans on the Mainland in leadership positions. The cultural value to not boast or call attention to yourself, to be part of a community or group — the negative side of it is that the American way to get ahead is that you *do* speak up; you *do* talk about yourself. The one thing that I hope comes out of this discussion of values is how that value can be dealt with differently, in a political sense, or in a leadership sense, by the *Nisei* who were successful.

George, Dan and Fuj, you all have been in leadership positions. Yet, so many of our *Sansei* went into professions that were "safe." They're professionals — they became lawyers and doctors and accountants and so forth. If we look at the high education level of Japanese Americans — the *Nisei, Sansei* and, now, the *Yonsei* — and we compare that with the numbers of Japanese Americans who are in senior positions at the top of Fortune 500 companies, running for political office, have considered running for office or are in major mainstream positions, the numbers are very, very low.

It is, perhaps, the reluctance to move beyond a certain point, of not wanting to assume a leadership role that remains a challenge. I believe it's possible to combine the values that the *Issei* and the *Nisei* taught the *Sansei* and take the positive aspects of those values and continue them, and yet incorporate other American values that may seem at odds with each other but that encourage more of our young people to feel that they can succeed in leadership positions. They are very successful from a professional standpoint, but all the data about who's in leadership does not include Japanese Americans.

Many *Nisei* ask me why we don't have younger Japanese Americans running for office, for example, particularly on the Mainland. In Hawai'i, you have many Japanese Americans in elected positions, but on the Mainland, we've had very few. Recent studies show that the numbers of Asian Americans that are on corporate boards and foundation boards are also very few. Yet we have so many Japanese Americans who are very, very talented. So there's something in that transmission of our values that has caused Japanese Americans to be too modest or too reluctant in some ways. I hope that the *Nisei* — those of you around this table — will encourage more of our *Yonsei*, and our *Gosei* generation, to not be afraid to step up and take leadership positions, because how we were brought up and how we do our work is a reflection of our values.

When I take Japanese Americans to Japan, there's something that makes them feel connected to Japan that is part of that value system that they grew up with. They feel something that is familiar. When other visitors go to Japan, they comment that there is something unique about the Japanese and that they have a respect for the Japanese people that's very different from when you go to other countries in Asia. I hope that beyond just a discussion of "What are those values?" — that there is encouragement that all of you can share that will be inspiring to our younger people.

Governor Ariyoshi: Irene, I think what you are doing is very important — your work now, the Japanese leadership group. It's not just an opportunity for Japanese Americans to meet with Japanese. What you do for individuals who become part of that group, the American Japanese, who begin to feel that, hey, they're more than just what they were doing. To me, that's a very valuable part of the work that you do.

Irene Hirano Inouye (agreeing): But it's helpful, George, when you and Dan and others share your experiences so that they hear, firsthand, why you believe that's important, and encourage them to do that. The fact that we have so many *Nisei* that excelled, despite all of the challenges that you had to face, is the legacy that I hope we can leave for our young people. There is a sense of pride about being of Japanese ancestry, and the experience of the 442nd and what happened in the camps is one important story. But it's also the "post-" story — the fact that so many of you went on to assume major leadership positions, despite all that you had to go through. When the *Sansei* and the *Yonsei* look at your post-World War II stories and when they read your words and hear your stories, that's what can inspire them — that they can do anything, since they didn't have the same kinds of barriers that you all faced.

Governor Ariyoshi: You know, I have a [note]pad for each of my grandchildren, and whenever I think about something that I think is hard for me to talk to them about, like values my parents taught me, but if I can talk about those things in relation to some activity that happened and how those values has made me make certain kinds of decisions, to me, it's going to be very valuable to my grandchildren, so I'm doing this kind of writing for them. It's very personal; I've not done it to my own children, but I'm beginning to do it for my grandchildren, because I want them to understand what they are a part of; the values that are a part of us can play a vital role in helping them in everything, in things that they do. So, I'm trying to give very specific examples to them — how values came about and me making certain decisions and doing certain things.

Fujio Matsuda: Now, to the point you made and maybe this pertains to that point. I remember my mother telling me when I was growing up, "*No aru taka wa tsume wo kakusei,*" (which meant) "The smart falcon doesn't show its claws" — another way of maybe saying, "Don't brag about things," or, I know so much, etc. So, maybe if that's the Japanese way of thinking about some of these things… Maybe people say that they don't want to show off, like in a classroom. Typically, in Hawai'i, at least, you have a classroom of twenty-five kids and a teacher asks a question, "Who knows the answer?" Very few Japanese hands will go up, even though they know the answer! So, maybe that's some manifestation of that kind of thinking.

Irene Hirano Inouye: Yes, I think so.

Ted Tsukiyama: Irene is saying that we've allowed humility and *enryo* (modestly refrain) to become almost a fault . . .

Irene Hirano Inouye: Yes, but "fault" is not the right word (laughter). I think it's about the situation, when you apply that — there's an appropriate time to respect one's culture and values, and there are other times when you have to speak up. You have to let people know that you have certain skills and talents.

Reverend Fujitani: As I was about to say, all good things have to come to an end, and our time is up.

~

The Reverend Ryokan Ara is the Bishop of the Tendai Mission in Hawai'i. Bishop Ara was born in Fukushima, Japan, and entered the Buddhist priesthood at the age of ten. He graduated from Taisho University, where he studied Tendai Buddhism.

Bishop Ara served at various temples in the Fukushima area before moving to Hawai'i in the early 1970s to establish the Tendai Mission of Hawai'i. In 1975, he started the Hawaii Ichigu Kai — the Hawai'i Chapter of the "One Corner Association," a service organization based on Buddhist philosophy and teachings. He also established the Hawaii Bijutsuin (Hawaii Institute of Arts), where Japanese cultural arts such as calligraphy, *ikebana*, Japanese-style painting and tea ceremony were taught.

Bishop Ara is a gifted and self-taught artist whose unique paintings of Buddha often combine Buddhist motifs with words of wisdom. His paintings have been exhibited in San Francisco, Boston and New York, as well as in Australia and, annually, in Japan.

In the 1990s, he initiated the first Honolulu *tōrō nagashi*, or floating lantern ceremony, on the Ala Wai Canal to remember departed loved ones.

In 2011, the Government of Japan presented Bishop Ara the Foreign Minister's Commendation. The award is presented to individuals who have made outstanding contributions to the promotion of mutual understanding and friendly relations between Japan and other foreign countries. Bishop Ara and his wife Kyoko raised two adult children.

Governor George R. Ariyoshi was elected America's first governor of Asian ancestry in 1974 and served until 1986 — an unprecedented three terms. When Governor John A. Burns became ill in 1973, then-Lieutenant Governor Ariyoshi was elevated to Acting Governor and completed the term of Burns, his longtime political mentor.

Ariyoshi graduated from McKinley High School and attended the University of Hawai'i. He graduated from Michigan State University and Michigan State Law School. A veteran of the Military Intelligence Service, Governor Ariyoshi's political career spanned more than three decades, beginning with his election to the Territorial House of Representatives, the Territorial and later State Senate and culminated with his election as the third Governor of the State of Hawai'i.

Since leaving office, Governor Ariyoshi has shared his time and expertise with many community, educational and business organizations, among them the East-West Center. He served on the Center's Board of Governors from 1995 to 2003, six of those years as Board Chair.

Governor Ariyoshi has been awarded honorary doctorates from several international universities. In 1997, he published his autobiography, "With Obligation to All."

In 1985, the Government of Japan awarded Governor Ariyoshi the Grand Cordon of the Sacred Treasure, First Class, and in 1987, he was presented the Emperor's Silver Cup.

Governor Ariyoshi was honored by the Pacific Buddhist Academy in 2010 at its "Lighting Our Way" recognition awards program. In 2012, the East-West Center presented its Asia Pacific Community Building Award to Governor Ariyoshi in recognition of his dedication to strengthening the bonds of understanding among the peoples and nations of Asia, the Pacific and the United States.

Governor Ariyoshi and his wife Jean are the parents of three adult children.

United States Senator Daniel K. Inouye was the first American of Japanese ancestry elected to the U.S. Congress. He first ran for elective office in 1954, winning election to the Hawai'i Territorial House of Representatives and, in 1958, the Territorial Senate. In 1959, Senator Inouye became Hawai'i's first elected member of the United States House of Representatives. He was elected to the U.S. Senate in 1962.

Senator Inouye attended public schools and graduated from McKinley High School. When the U.S. War Department authorized the formation of an all-Japanese American volunteer Army unit, the 442nd Regimental Combat Team, Inouye was among the 10,000 from Hawai'i who stepped forward to fight for America. He was seventeen years old at the time.

Daniel Inouye's dreams of becoming a surgeon were dashed forever when his right arm was shattered in a grenade blast in Italy. The injury was so severe that his arm had to be amputated. Inouye decided to make the law his career.

After receiving his Bachelor's degree from the University of Hawai'i, he went on to George Washington University Law School in Washington, D.C., where he earned his law degree. In 2008, George Washington University awarded Senator Inouye an honorary Doctor of Laws.

Senator Inouye was asked to deliver the keynote address at the 1968 Democratic

National Convention. He served as a member of the Senate Watergate Committee and, subsequently, chaired a special committee that investigated the Iran-Contra affair.

In June 2000, Senator Inouye was among twenty Japanese American World War II soldiers who had served in the 100th Infantry Battalion/442nd Regimental Combat Team to whom President Bill Clinton presented Medals of Honor, the nation's highest award for valor, after their Distinguished Service Cross citations were reviewed and upgraded to Medal of Honor.

In 1999, Senator Inouye was awarded The Grand Cordon of the Order of the Rising Sun, by the Government of Japan, in recognition of his contributions to enhancing the relationship between the U.S. and Japan as a "pioneer" in the U.S. Congress.

In 2011, the Government of Japan honored Senator Inouye's contributions to enhancing goodwill and understanding between Japan and the United States by awarding him a second Imperial Decoration, The Grand Cordon of the Order of the Paulownia Flowers. Senator Inouye was the first foreigner of Japanese ancestry to receive the honor, which is the highest level of National Orders that a non-Japanese citizen can receive.

Senator Inouye succumbed to complications from a respiratory illness on December 17, 2012, at the age of eighty-eight. At the time of his passing, he was the nation's longest-serving Senator and the Senate's Pro Tempore, placing him third in line to the U.S. presidency.

In August 2013, the White House announced that Senator Inouye was among sixteen Americans who had been selected to receive the Presidential Medal of Freedom, the nation's highest civilian honor. President Barack Obama will present the award to Senator Inouye posthumously later this year. The Presidential Medal of Freedom was established fifty years ago by President John F. Kennedy to recognize individuals who have made "especially meritorious contributions to the security or national interests of the United States, to world peace, or to cultural or other significant public or private endeavors."

Senator Inouye's first wife, Margaret "Maggie," with whom he had a son, Ken, died of cancer in 2006. At the time of his passing, Senator Inouye was married to Irene Hirano Inouye, whom he wed in 2008.

Irene Hirano Inouye is the President of the U.S.-Japan Council, which was established in 2009 to build people-to-people relationships between the two countries. The U.S.-Japan Council is headquartered in Washington, D.C. Through her work at the Council, Hirano Inouye also administers the TOMODACHI Initiative, a public-private partnership with the U.S. Embassy in Tōkyō that invests in young Japanese and Americans while supporting the recovery of the Tōhōku region from the March 2011 earthquake, tsunami and nuclear disaster. In her role as President of the U.S.-Japan Council, Hirano Inouye also leads the Japanese American Leadership Delegation, a select group of Japanese American leaders from across the United States, to Japan to engage with Japanese leaders.

Hirano Inouye was previously the President and Chief Executive Officer of the Japanese American National Museum, which she led for twenty years. The National Museum works to promote understanding and appreciation of America's ethnic and cultural diversity by sharing the Japanese American experience through exhibitions and public programs. As President of the Japanese American National Museum, Hirano Inouye was instrumental in ensuring that the story of Hawai'i's Japanese Americans — from immigration to World War II to contemporary society — was included in the overall Japanese American story.

Hirano Inouye also served as President and CEO of the National Center for the Preservation of Democracy, which is affiliated with the Japanese American National Museum.

Hirano Inouye chairs the Ford Foundation's Board of Trustees. She also serves as a Trustee of the Kresge Foundation, which is committed to providing opportunity for low-income people; The Washington Center for Internships and Academic Seminars; and the Independent Sector. In Hawai'i, Hirano Inouye serves as a member of the advisory board of the APDR3 Asia-Pacific Disaster Risk Reduction and Resiliency Network of the University of Hawai'i Foundation.

Irene Hirano Inouye was married to the late U.S. Senator Daniel K. Inouye and has one adult daughter. After her husband's passing, Hirano Inouye established the Daniel K. Inouye Memorial Fund to assist the organizations and causes that Senator Inouye supported during his life.

Consul General Yoshihiko Kamo was born in Shizuoka, Japan, and has represented the Government of Japan in Bangladesh, Thailand, Canada, Myanmar and Finland. He served as the Consul General in Houston, Texas, prior to being assigned as Consul General of Hawai'i and American Samoa in August 2009. In August 2012, Japan's Ministry of Foreign Affairs appointed him the country's Ambassador to the United Arab Emirates. Mr. Kamo and his wife Etsuko are the parents of two daughters.

The Zadankai discussants exchange thoughts and ideas in U.S. Senator Daniel K. Inouye's office in the Prince Kūhiō Federal Building in Honolulu on July 6, 2012. Clockwise from top right: Senator Inouye, former Hawai'i Governor George R. Ariyoshi, then-Consul General of Japan Yoshihiko Kamo (back to camera), Bishop Ryokan Ara, Ted Tsukiyama, Irene Hirano Inouye, the Reverend Yoshiaki Fujitani and Dr. Fujio Matsuda. Observing the discussion in the background is Peter Boylan, Senator Inouye's Deputy Chief of Staff.

The July 6, 2012, Zadankai discussants gathered for a group photo. Seated, from left: Irene Hirano Inouye, U.S. Senator Daniel K. Inouye and former Hawai'i Governor George R. Ariyoshi. Standing from left: Ted Tsukiyama, Dr. Fujio Matsuda, the Reverend Yoshiaki Fujitani, Bishop Ryokan Ara and then-Consul General of Japan Yoshihiko Kamo.

"SHOW ME WHAT KIND OF PERSON YOU ARE…"

Wallace S. Fujiyama

"Going to college is tough enough as it is, but when you encounter a professor who can't speak plain English, who doesn't even enunciate or who doesn't speak at a level that students can understand, it's very tough…We have 'minimum qualifications' for this position and 'minimum qualifications' for that position and applicants look very nice — on paper. But I would tell you this: Don't tell me what you have published. Don't tell me how many jobs you have had. Show me, instead, what kind of person you are. Show me how your character is going to be good for this institution and the students it serves. You can be smart as a whip, but if you lack character, you're an absolute zero in my book…"

— *Source: Honolulu attorney and University of Hawaiʻi Board of Regents member Wallace S. "Wally" Fujiyama as quoted in the February 20, 1982, edition of* The Honolulu Advertiser.

GLOSSARY

ENGLISH

GI: Abbreviation for "Government Issue," meaning supplied by the U.S. military. The term also became a reference to veterans or members of the U.S. armed forces, particularly those serving in the Army.

GI Bill (or *GI Bill of Rights*): Enacted officially as the Servicemen's Readjustment Act of 1944, this landmark educational benefits program has been heralded as one of the most significant pieces of legislation produced by the federal government to address the need for jobs for millions of returning World War II veterans. The GI Bill helped pay for college education and vocational training for veterans. It also provided home, farm and business loan benefits, as well as unemployment benefits. The majority of the veterans took advantage of the educational benefits, including large numbers of *Nisei* from Hawai'i, who went on to become doctors; lawyers and, some, eventually, judges; school teachers and professors; lawmakers and even members of Congress. Others used the vocational training it provided to learn trades such as optometry, watchmaking, etc. In its peak year, 1949, veterans accounted for nearly half of all college admissions. By the time the original GI Bill ended in July 1956, 7.8 million of the 16 million World War II veterans had utilized the GI Bill. The bill was revamped in 1984 as the Montgomery GI Bill. The program is administered by the U.S. Department of Veterans Affairs. *(Source: www.gibill.va.gov/benefits/history_timeline)*

kiku ointment: A salve made from the petals of the chrysanthemum flower (*kiku* in Japanese) and applied to skin irritations.

Meiji-era: The period in Japan from 1868 through 1912. The *Meiji* era saw the restoration of Emperor Meiji to the throne, the end of the *daimyo* (territorial lords) and their *samurai* (warrior) retainers, and the beginning of modern industrial Japan. Emperor Meiji's reign was marked by international adventures which involved wars with China and Russia and control over the Korean Peninsula, Formosa (Taiwan), the Ryūkyū Islands (Okinawa) and Manchuria.

Pidgin or *Pidgin English:* Hawaiʻi Creole (or Hawaiʻi Creole English) is usually referred to as "Pidgin" or "Pidgin English." Its rich linguistic history is rooted in Hawaiʻi's plantation era, when a common language developed from the spoken native languages of the various immigrant groups. *(Source: www.hawaii.edu/ satocenter/langnet/definitions/hce.html)*

Territory of Hawaiʻi: Hawaiʻi was a Territory of the United States prior to being admitted as the fiftieth State of the union on August 21, 1959. In 1900, Hawaiʻi became a U.S. Territory after having been annexed by the United States in 1898. Sanford B. Dole, a lawyer whose father had arrived in the Islands as a missionary, was appointed Hawaiʻi's first Territorial Governor by President William McKinley. Dole had spearheaded the overthrow of Hawaiʻi's monarchy in 1893. Hawaiʻi's road to Statehood and full representation for its citizens nearly six decades later was engineered by the future Governor of Hawaiʻi, John A. Burns. *(Source: history. state.gov/milestones/1866-1898/Hawaii)*

HAWAIIAN

aloha: A special word with many meanings: hello, good-bye, love. The aloha spirit represents warmth, openness, friendship, acceptance, caring.

hānai: Native Hawaiian practice of fostering or informally adopting a child.

haole: A white Caucasian.

hapa: A person of mixed race or ethnicity.

hula: Hawaiʻi's cultural dance. There are two styles of hula — hula *kahiko*, or ancient hula, and hula *ʻauwana*, which is modern hula.

kalo: Taro, a nutrient-rich starchy plant.

loʻi: A field of planted *kalo*, or taro.

makule: Aged, elderly person or people. (The Makule League is a popular softball league among elderly players .)

ʻohā: The young plant shoots of the *kalo*, or taro, plant

ʻohana: Family

JAPANESE

aburage: Deep-fried *tōfu* (soybean curd)

aikidō: The Japanese art of self-defense. *Aikidō* emphasizes the importance of achieving complete mental calm and control of one's body to overcome an opponent's attack. *Aikidō* traces its origins to Japanese martial traditions of *jūdō* and *kendō*. It was developed in its modern form in the early 20th century by Ueshiba Morihei.

beiju: Eighty-eighth birthday — an auspicious birthday for a person who has lived to be eighty-eight years old.

benkyō: The act of studying.

bonsai: A miniature potted tree, usually pine, depicting nature.

chōnan: Eldest son.

chan: Affectionate suffix for a child (i.e., Koko-*chan*) or a loved one (i.e., *Obaa-chan, Ojii-chan*).

chūgi: Loyalty.

Dana: An ancient Buddhist concept from India meaning "selfless giving," or giving without expectation of receiving something in return. Hawai'i's Project Dana is based on the precept of selfless giving.

dōjō: Martial arts practice hall.

doryoku: To endeavor, to strive to do one's best, diligence.

eta: Outcast, or untouchable people who were condemned to do "dirty" work, such as slaughtering animals, handling corpses and other tasks that no one else would do; the modern-era term is *burakumin*.

furoba: Bathhouse.

gakkō: School.

gakumon: Education.

gaman: To endure hardship in silence.

gambare (or *gambari, ganbare*), *gambaru:* To persevere, persistence.

gimu: Duty.

giri: Duty, obligation.

haji: Shame.

haji okosanai yo ni: Translated, do not bring shame.

Issei: First-generation immigrants from Japan.

jūdō: A modern martial art created in Japan in 1882 by Jigoro Kano to harmoniously develop the intellectual, moral and physical aspects of young people. *Jūdō*, which means "soft or flexible way," is the efficient use of your opponent's strength and momentum to defeat him. *Jūdō* was accepted as an Olympic sport in 1964.

kansha: Gratitude.

kantoku: Superintendent.

kappa: Raincoat.

Kimigayo: The title of the national anthem of post-1868 Japan. The lyrics to "*Kimigayo*" are based on a *waka* (literally, Japanese poem) that was written during Japan's Heian Period (794–1185). The anthem is sung to a melody that was written in the Imperial Period (1868–1945). *(Source: www.princeton.edu)*

kimono: Traditional Japanese long-sleeved garment made of precious textiles, such as silk or brocade. In most Hawai'i homes, they were folded and stored in cedar chests *(tansu).*

konnyaku: Traditional Japanese food ingredient made from the corm of the *konnyaku* potato, or konjac plant (*Amorphophallus konjac*), also known as the Devil's Tongue plant.

koseki tōhon: Japanese family registry.

kyōryoku: Cooperation; working together.

manjū: Baked or steamed bun filled with sweetened, mashed beans.

meiyo: Honor.

moyashi: Bean sprouts.

Namo Amida Butsu: From the Buddhist scripture, "Homage to the Most Compassionate One." *Namo* is sometimes spelled *Namu* — both spellings are correct.

nasake: Compassion.

Nihon wa erai kuni desu: Translated, Japan is a great country.

Nikkeijin, or nikkei: Person of Japanese ancestry born outside of Japan.

Nisei: Second-generation children of immigrants from Japan.

Obaa-chan: Affectionate name for Grandmother.

oba-san: Older woman.

obon (also *bon*): Annual observance during the summer months when Buddhists welcome home the spirits of their ancestors. *Bon* dances with lively music, food and dancing are held at Buddhist temples to honor the ancestors until they must return to the spirit world. *Bon* dances in Hawai'i attract participants of all ethnic and religious backgrounds.

ohana: Honorific term for flower, or flower arrangement.

oji-san: Older man.

Ojii-chan: Affectionate name for Grandfather.

Okaasan: Mother.

okaeshi: To return a favor or reciprocate after receiving a gift.

okagesama de: With gratitude for your support.

omoiyari: Consideration of others.

on: Obligation and a debt of gratitude in the deepest sense; kindness.

origami: Literally, folding paper. The traditional Japanese art of folding paper into shapes such as flowers, animals and other items.

Otoosan: Father.

oyakōkō: Love your parents, filial piety.

samurai: Japanese warrior.

Sansei, Yonsei, Gosei: Respectively, the third, fourth and fifth generation offspring of immigrants from Japan.

sekinin: Responsibility.

senbei: Japanese crackers for snacking.

sensei: Teacher; also a respectful way to address an individual of stature, such as a minister (i.e., Ara-*Sensei*).

shikata ga nai: Cannot be helped, nothing can be done; acceptance with resignation.

shinbō: Patience.

shi-on: The Four Gratitudes or Obligations: gratitude to parents, to one's country, to all beings and to the Buddha.

shōjiki: Honesty.

shūshin: Moral training, literally, to arrange or correct the inner self.

sonkei: Respect, especially of elders and teachers.

sumotori: Sumo wrestler.

tanomoshi: A community-based credit system used by the *Issei* and early *Nisei* generations for small, short-term loans, or to earn a small interest from the *tanomoshi*. It operated like a finance company with unique rules. The members of the *tanomoshi* consisted usually of trusted friends. *Tanomoshi* was especially helpful in Hawai'i because most Japanese could not get short-term loans from *haole*-operated financial institutions. These days, many younger AJAs organize *tanomoshi* groups for socialization purposes rather than for financial reasons. (For a detailed description of *tanomoshi*, see "Kodomo no Tame Ni" by Dr. Dennis Ogawa.)

tansu: Japanese-style chest of drawers.

tōfu: Soybean curd cakes.

tsunami: A series of strong ocean waves generated by an earthquake.

Uchinanchu: Okinawan language term for a person of Okinawan ancestry.

udon: Thick Japanese noodles.

wa: Harmony and peace.

yāninju: Okinawan language term for family cohesiveness.

yarikata: The way one does things.

zadankai: A conversation; a "talk story."

CHINESE

Qigong (pronounced *chee-gung*): An ancient Chinese healthcare system that integrates physical postures, breathing techniques and focused intention. Translated, *chi* usually means the life force or vital energy that flows through everything in the universe. *Gong* means accomplishment, or skill cultivated through steady practice. *(Source: nqa.org/resources.what-is-qigong)*

INDIAN

Bodhisattva: One who compassionately refrains from entering *nirvana*, or a state of enlightenment or eternal bliss, in order to save others from reincarnation. *Bodhisattvas*, which is a Sanskrit spelling, serve as eternal helpers of the Buddha, embodying his boundless compassion and mercy. *(Source: artic.edu/aic/collections/exhibitions/Indian/Bodhisattva)*

PIDGIN

kotonk: Slang term devised by Hawai'i *Nisei* soldiers for their Mainland counterparts during military training in World War II. Hawai'i *Nisei* were referred to as "Buddhaheads." Over time, the early derogatory nature of the terms evolved into simply a way of distinguishing Mainland from Hawai'i *Nisei* soldiers.

portagee: Derogatory reference to the Portuguese ethnic group or to a person of Portuguese ancestry.

pake (pronounced *pah-kay*): Derogatory reference to the Chinese ethnicity or to a person of Chinese ancestry; also a derogatory reference to someone who is frugal or stingy.

INDEX